John Sh[illegible]

A Holy Rebellion

THOMAS ICE
ROBERT DEAN, JR.

HARVEST HOUSE PUBLISHERS
Eugene, Oregon 97402

Except where otherwise indicated, all Scripture quotations in this book are taken from the New American Standard Bible, © 1960, 1962, 1963, 1968, 1971, 1972, 1973, 1975, 1977 by the Lockman Foundation. Used by permission.

Verses marked KJV are taken from the King James Version of the Bible.

A HOLY REBELLION

Eugene, Oregon 97402

Library of Congress Cataloging-in-Publication Data

Ice, Thomas.
A holy rebellion : a strategy for spiritual warfare / Thomas Ice, Robert Dean, Jr.
ISBN 0-89081-805-3
1. Devil 2. Demonology. 3. Spirituality. I. Dean, Robert, 1952- . II. Title.
BT981.I34 1990 90-35505
CIP

Printed in the United States of America.

To our parents

Alton and Vesta Ice

Bob and Gloria Dean

who fought the good fight by leading us to a saving knowledge of Jesus Christ and whose love and support through the years has enabled us to fight the good fight. We love you.

Train up a child in the way he should go, and even when he is old he will not depart from it.

—Proverbs 22:6

Acknowledgments

No book is ever produced without the help and support of a number of people. We want to thank Christine Kim, Erica Miller, Betty Sears, and Karen Peterson for their helpful comments and suggestions on different portions of the manuscript. Dr. Charles Ryrie provided helpful suggestions as well as someone to talk to as we sought to refine our understanding of the Scriptures. Eileen Mason, chief editor at Harvest House, gave innumerable suggestions. Thanks, Eileen! We are also grateful to our respective churches for giving us the freedom and time to work on this book. Finally, we wish to thank Grace Bible Church in San Marcos, as well as Gordon and David Whitelock and the folks at Camp Peniel, who provided us with places to retreat from the pressing demands of our churches so we could write. Without the help of all these people we would still be on Chapter 1!

Contents

A Holy Rebellion

– 1 –

THE GREAT WAR

Another long, miserable day at work—and now this. Someone's car had overheated and blocked one of the three lanes left open on the freeway while the others were under construction. Sue was steamed. Not only had her day at the office been an absolute disaster, but now she had to put up with this. She was going to be at least an hour late getting to the daycare center to pick up Joey, but the extra bills from the air-conditioner repair left her with no extra money to eat out on. After a day like this Sue dreaded having to fix dinner when she got home. She felt so trapped. She couldn't understand why life wasn't going better now that she was a Christian.

For the last several months it seemed that so many things had gone wrong. First the car needed a valve job, then Joey broke his arm so badly that it needed to be surgically set, and then the compressor on her air conditioner went out. She couldn't believe how the bills had mounted up. It would take her at least a year, and maybe two, to get all these bills paid off. And she knew that in the meantime other unexpected expenses were sure to come up. She really needed something to perk up her spirits right now.

While she was waiting in traffic she decided to turn on the radio; maybe that would help. That's when she heard it—an advertisement for the new steak restaurant which had just opened. As she thought about it, she dreamed of how great it would be if she could just pick Joey up and go there for a nice big steak and a good, rich dessert. But she knew she couldn't afford a meal like this and ought to put it right out of her mind. But that gnawing voice inside her said she was worth it. After all, what difference would another 30 dollars or so mean on her credit card? She was worth it! She would face the money problems later on.

Is this a valid response to the pressures and circumstances in life? Or could it be that the small voice is really the influence of the world system? What could Sue do to avoid this kind of thinking?

Can Prayer Exorcise a City?

Jose and Maria had been born-again Christians for only two years. During that time they had become quite involved in their church. For several months the pastor had been teaching about spiritual warfare, especially prayer. One of his major emphases was that Satan and his demons held sway over certain territories, and that in Miami (where they lived) one of the reasons there was so much drug traffic, prostitution, and violence was because of the demonic oppression of the city. If Miami were ever to be freed from the dominion of these demons, then Christians must gather together and pray. Only through the effective prayer of the Christians would the holy angels have the power to gain victory over the demons and enable Miami to experience spiritual revival.

The series on spiritual warfare culminated with a weeklong prayer vigil. People in the church had been encouraged and challenged to join six- and ten-hour prayer vigils and to pray and fast around the clock. At the end of the week, words of prophecy were spoken in the church encouraging the people that their prayers had been effective and that many of the demons had been routed.

Jose and Maria lived in the Colombian sector of Miami, and many of their friends and family members were involved in the drug trade. Jose and Maria were excited that this deliverance would give them the opportunity to witness to family members without hindrance from satanic opposition.

When their words of witness were met with the same familiar hostility they did not question, but waited in faith. Yet as the days went by they noticed that there was very little difference in the moral climate of Miami. The drug traffic continued, immorality was just as rampant, and gunfire continued to punctuate the night air.

Can prayer deliver a city or neighborhood from the influence of demons?

Can Christians Be Demon-Possessed?

Julia was in her mid-forties. She was divorced, and she struggled to raise her two children on a single income. Yet she was always confident that God would provide. Life had been difficult, but the one hope that carried her through was her sincere hope in God. Yet in spite of this hope, for over ten years now she had struggled with bouts of depression, and had finally started visiting counselors. Over the last five years she had seen three counselors, but the depression continued.

One weekend a visiting speaker at her church taught that Christians could be demon-possessed. Julia had always been taught that a Christian could not be possessed, but the speaker said that depression could be a sign of possession. She left church that night with a mixed sense of relief and fear—relief because now she might know her real problem, and fear because now she believed her depression might be the result of demonic possession. But she wasn't sure just what to do about all this.

Can Christians be demon-possessed? What is the difference between demon *possession* and demon *influence*?

Can Christians Be Cursed?

Frank and Martha were finally getting away for a weekend "second honeymoon" together, even though it meant leaving their high-school-age daughter at home alone. They trusted Linda because she had never given them any real reason to doubt her. Now that she was about to graduate from high school, they believed the time had come to give her the opportunity to show her maturity. But unknown to them, Linda had planned to have a party the whole time they were gone. During the party a group of her friends who were involved in a Satanic rock music group and a cult hid a pentagram in a junk drawer in the kitchen and placed a curse on the family.

Several days after Frank and Martha returned home they sensed that something was different about their life, but they couldn't put their finger on it. During the following weeks they noticed a deterioration in the circumstances of their lives. Several things went wrong with their car, and the air conditioner in their home had to be completely replaced. They also began to notice more bickering among the family members and a certain spiritual confusion in the family.

About this time Frank heard from his neighbor that there had been quite a bit of traffic in and out of their house while they had been away. Eventually the entire story came out, including the identification of some of the kids as members of a Satanist cult. When Frank told a friend about all of this, his friend suggested that the reason things were not going well for the family was because the Satanists had probably put a curse on the house, and the family would have to undergo some sort of exorcism before they could be delivered. This sounded more like superstitious nonsense to Frank than sensible advice, but he began to wonder what the Bible taught about demons, curses, and spells.

Can Christians be victims of occultic curses?

Will Mind Control Help You?

Carl was a very successful salesman. At 25 years of age his commissions for the past year had earned him almost 200,000 dollars. Furthermore, he was being considered for a sales manager position. Carl was overwhelmed by God's blessing in his life.

One day the senior manager of his division called him into his office. He praised Carl for his work and ambition and saw nothing but the best for him. However, he suggested one particular seminar that Carl should attend if he was to ever reach his goals. He implied that Carl would probably not receive the promotion unless he attended.

As Carl questioned his manager about the seminar he discovered that it was designed to teach him mind-control principles, improve his memory, and enable him to influence other people in a good way. One of the most important results of the seminar, Carl's manager told him, was that he would be introduced to a spiritual counselor upon whom he could rely and who would give him an added edge over his competition.

Is Carl on the verge of being involved in occultic practices disguised as sales techniques? Is mind control (Positive Mental Attitude) a biblical approach to handling life's challenges?

Can Demons Make You Sin?

Bob and his sister Susan had grown up in a Christian home and had been well trained in the Scriptures. However, when Susan was in college she began to lose her spiritual bearings and became lukewarm toward God. For several years Bob had been praying for her, and it seemed that God had answered his prayers. Susan had joined a new church that was quite alive, and she was more turned on to Jesus then ever before.

This so impressed Bob that he soon joined this same church as well. He was impressed that these people seemed to act aggressively on their faith and truly expected God to perform miracles and signs and wonders just as He did in the New Testament. At first Bob was skeptical, but he heard so many glowing testimonies from Christians delivered from demons and now free from sins that had plagued them that he too was thinking that perhaps the problems he faced with sin were the result of demonic influence in his life.

Can demons (spirits of lust, murder, anger, etc.) cause Christians to sin, or is sin simply the result of our own sin nature?

Can You Have a Demon of Lust?

Bill had been introduced to pornography as a young teen. Through the years it had become more and more of an obsession. This intensified in college when he began looking for more ways to get his sexual thrills and discovered adult peep shows. While a senior in college he was led to the Lord through a campus ministry, and for several years the porno problem no longer bothered him. But after he was married he again found himself tempted by the pleasures of the porn palace and the massage parlor. What made this situation so difficult for him was that he was in his second year of seminary, studying to be a pastor. He just couldn't understand why he could not overcome this sin.

Finally the guilt became so great that Bill went to one of his seminary professors for advice. This professor suggested that it was very likely that he was being influenced by a demon of lust, and that he should go through a deliverance session to gain freedom from this demon.

Do demons cause specific sins in people's lives? How are Christians to defeat the sins of the flesh?

Can Pagan Objects Haunt You?

Fred and Linda had been on the missionary committee at their church for 20 years. Now that Fred was finally retired, they went overseas to visit several of the church missionaries. When they returned home they brought with them a number of artifacts with which they hoped to help people in their church understand the various cultures where their missionaries served. So they set these objects up in a mission display in the basement of the church. But soon a lady in the church confronted them by saying that some of the objects they brought back were used in pagan rituals or were idols, and that Fred and Linda needed to destroy these things and cleanse the church before they became victims of the demons associated with them.

Can Christians who are walking with the Lord in obedience innocently or unknowingly pick up demons through objects associated with occult practices, and if so, what should they do about it?

Can You Inherit a Demon?

Sandy had grown up in a family that was deeply entrenched in occultic practices and witchcraft. Both her parents were in a coven which her grandfather had founded. Her mother was also a palm-reader and astrologer. Her father had on a number of occasions served as a channel for the spirit of a man who had allegedly lived in India 20,000 years ago. Because of Sandy's upbringing, this was all she knew about religion.

When Sandy left home in her late teen years to attend college, her roommate, an evangelical Christian, began to talk to her about Jesus Christ, who died for her sins. Sandy's roommate explained to her what the Bible taught about Satan, demons, witchcraft, and astrology. At first Sandy was hostile, but during the semester she accepted the challenge to read the Bible for herself. Under the guidance of her roommate she came to see that what she knew as religion would never provide eternal life and that she must trust in Jesus Christ alone for her salvation.

After Sandy was saved she began attending a large church in town. Because of her background she still had many questions about her new faith and the witchcraft she had left behind. Her roommate suggested that she go to one of the counselors in the church for answers. The counselor told her that trusting in Christ alone as her Savior was not enough. Because Sandy had come from such an occultic background, she needed to renounce all of these practices and very possibly needed deliverance from the demons she inherited through her family.

Does the Bible teach that a person saved out of an occultic background can have a demon that was passed on from one generation to another? Must such a person not only turn completely to Christ but also be delivered from these inherited demons as a separate step?

You Are at War

Each of the stories you have just read is based on a true incident, and each represents a cross-section of what is happening in the lives of many people today. Each one of these Christians wants to live a life pleasing to God, yet each faces daily struggles and opposition in his or her walk with the Lord. People who are living in Satan's world, but who have given their allegiance to God, are warriors in rebellion against Satan. They are in every sense of the word *holy rebels*. This is the essence of spiritual warfare.

If you are a believer in the Lord Jesus Christ as your Savior, then you too have declared rebellion against Satan. Maybe you didn't realize this; maybe you're not aware that the Bible teaches that Satan is the prince of the power of the air (Ephesians 2:2) and the god of this age (2 Corinthians 4:4), and that before you were saved Satan was at work in you as one of the sons of disobedience (Ephesians 2:2). Once you were saved you became a significant soldier in the greatest war ever fought, a spiritual war fought between the power of God (light) and the forces of Satan (darkness). As we will discover in the following pages, the Bible clearly teaches all of these truths. In addition, the Bible teaches that each believer must learn how to fight in the battle. The Bible is our combat manual, and in it we find the vital instructions we need in order to combat Satan and his two great allies, the world system and the sin nature.

In the coming pages we will look at each of these three enemies: the devil, the world, and the flesh. We will discover the great principles that God has given us to defeat these enemies in our personal lives. We will see more clearly the role that Christians are to play in this great spiritual drama. And we will come to understand that our knowledge of these teachings comprises the basics of the Christian life.

Watching the Game Films

Unfortunately, contemporary teaching on the great doctrine of spiritual warfare has caused Christians to focus almost exclusively on battles with Satan and demons. If this were truly the emphasis of Scripture, then there would be no problem. However, because this is *not* the primary focus of Scripture, but only one aspect of the teaching, then this overemphasis is misleading and even dangerous. It becomes dangerous when it causes Christians to focus on attacks and solutions in only one realm of spiritual warfare, leaving them vulnerable to attacks from the other two realms. The Bible clearly addresses spiritual warfare as taking place simultaneously on three battlefronts: the devil, the world, and the flesh. So must we.

Just as a football coach studies the game films of his opponent before the big game to discover his strategies and tactics, so Christians need to know the strategies, tactics, and abilities of their enemies before they can effectively rebel against them. In other words, we must understand the nature of the rebellion and who we are rebelling against before we can accurately understand what we should be doing. By examining the lives of the great saints and great spiritual battles of Scripture, we can see the strategies of the enemy and learn principles for avoiding the snares and assaults of the devil, the traps of worldliness, and the drive of our own sinful nature.

Once we understand the spiritual war that we are a part of, then we must decide what we are to do. How can we live in the world and not be worldly? How can we have victory over the lusts of the flesh? And what does it mean to resist the devil? We need biblical insight into how we will be attacked so that we will know what we are to do to protect ourselves.

The Highest Authority

Many Christians today are losing the battle in spiritual warfare because they do not have an adequate knowledge of God's Word. This has led some into occultic practices which have been cleverly disguised as "neutral" self-help techniques. Others have one foot in the world and the other in the Bible, and cannot understand why biblical principles don't seem to work for them. Defeat is commonplace because our lives are not established on truly biblical principles, but rather on the shifting foundation of man's experience.

As we have surveyed much of the contemporary literature written for Christians, we have discovered an extremely wide range of ideas, many of which are mutually contradictory. Both the issues and the solutions differ widely. We have read many fine-sounding discussions on spiritual warfare which did not have a biblical basis for the teaching. Some teach that Christians can be demon-possessed while others teach that they cannot. If one view is true, then Christians must live one way and the solutions to the problem must lie in one direction. If the other view is true, then the problems and solutions offered by the first view are irrelevant. How can we find our way out of this maze, and find timeless truth that we can base our lives on?

We believe that the Bible is our highest authority, and that only God has sufficient knowledge and understanding of both our enemies and our human nature to accurately inform us about spiritual conflict and what to do about it. The Christian must always be like those men and women of Berea who received the highest praise from the apostle Paul because they did not simply take his word, but searched the Scriptures daily to verify his teaching (Acts 17:11).

The Real Source of Truth

Many of the errors that have crept into the church, some of which have become very popular, are based on misunderstandings and misinterpretations of Scripture. Sometimes this happens because the writers have not taken into account the original languages of the Bible or have misused them. Therefore it is important that we occasionally refer to the original Greek and Hebrew wording of Scripture in order to more accurately interpret God's Word.

At other times error creeps in because we rely upon interpretations of experiences or personal testimony that may not be consistent with Scripture. This is especially so in the area of Satan and demons, and what they can do to Christians. Testimonies of missionaries working among pagan tribes where there is much demonic activity are used to support a particular line of teaching. How should these stories be evaluated, especially since some of these occurrences are used to support one position and others are used to support a contradictory position? Is it valid to appeal to these types of experiences to find truth?

Before we can ever hope to have victory over the sin and evil that are part of our universe, we must first understand the role of God's Word. Much of what is taught today contains testimonies of personal experience or the experiences of other people. We must find out how we are to regard such testimony, and we must continuously seek to determine a true, biblical approach to spiritual warfare. The failure to do this is one reason that so many believers are impotent in the warfare. They have either lost the sure foundation of the Word of God or they have severely weakened it by relying upon interpretations of experiences that run contradictory to what the Bible clearly teaches.

When you have finished reading this book we hope that you will understand the difference between the worldly, almost-superstitious views of Satan that have invaded many of our churches and a truly biblical perspective of evil and our calling to spiritual warfare. We pray that you will be armed with the truth of the Scriptures and will stand firm against the schemes of the devil and his great deception.

— 2 —

ULTIMATE INTELLIGENCE

The unfolding of Thy words gives light; it gives understanding to the simple.

—Psalm 119:130

During the Second World War one of the most important elements of the Allied victory was provided by the underground forces in the German-occupied countries. These groups kept tabs on the German units in their vicinity and relayed this information to Allied headquarters in London. In London, General Eisenhower's military intelligence staff would collate the information, which was then used to formulate strategy and tactics. Rarely did more than a handful of people have access to all of this information. The lower-level commanders and soldiers were told only what they needed to know in order to carry out their specific responsibilities. No soldier would ever have thought to ask for all the information available to Eisenhower so that he could verify the validity of his own orders or even understand why he was being ordered to carry out a particular mission.

Only God Knows

In the same way only God has a complete picture and full understanding of the warfare that takes place in the heavenlies. Christians are analogous to His footsoldiers. Our operations orders are given in the Scriptures. There we are told everything we need to know to successfully carry out our specific mission, which is the pursuit of godliness, holiness, or Christlikeness.

Unlike human armies, who face physical opponents, Christians face intangible and invisible opponents. Under normal conditions the enemy we wage war against cannot be perceived by human senses. The danger we face is to attempt to rely upon our own reason and experience to develop strategies for warfare. Since we know very little about the strengths, capabilities, and strategies of our opponents, and because we cannot see into that realm, we must rely totally upon the combat information given to us in the Scriptures. As in physical military conflict, God has not told us everything that is going on in these realms, but He *has* told us all that we need to know to protect ourselves and carry out our mission successfully. When we begin to rely on information based on sources other than the Bible, we may render ourselves vulnerable because we have unknowingly overstepped our bounds.

The apostle Paul writes in Ephesians 6:12, "Our struggle is not against flesh and blood, but against the rulers, against the powers, against the world forces of this darkness, against the spiritual forces of wickedness in the heavenly places." The struggle that Christians are in is not a *physical* struggle but a *spiritual* struggle. It is a struggle that ultimately is not against other human beings but is against the powers of darkness. Left to our own resources, we are totally blind and ignorant when it comes to knowing what the enemy is up to. How can we know what is going on when we are operating in the dark?

Not in the Dark

Especially when it involves the unseen spiritual forces of the demonic, we are operating in an arena in which we are virtually blind to all that is taking place around us. However, God is a loving God and has not left us in the dark to try to figure things out on our own. Just as God told Adam and Eve all they *needed to know* (but not all they *could have known*) in order for them to live for Him in the garden, so He has informed us in the Bible of everything we need to know about the powers of darkness. Not only does the Bible tell us about the struggle we are involved in, but if it were not for the Scriptures we would only be vaguely aware that we were even in a struggle in the first place. We would be severely limited by the weaknesses of our experience and our limited knowledge. God has not only given us the Bible, but He has also given Christians the Holy Spirit, who enlightens our minds so that we can understand the Bible, and on the basis of this knowledge exercise discernment in the decisions we make.

It is clear from Scripture that Christians are engaged in a struggle with unseen forces. Knowing this, several important questions should come to our minds: Who are these forces, these rulers, these powers, these world forces of darkness? What is their objective, and how do they operate? How can we identify them, how can we fight against them, and how can we be protected from them?

Today we are faced with much teaching about these demonic forces that cannot be derived from Scripture, but instead comes from the personal experiences of Christians. Is this source valid, or is Scripture all we need to successfully rebel against Satan?

The One True Source

The Bible itself claims to be our only source of certain knowledge about these forces that we are rebelling against. Not only does it claim to be the sole source of knowledge about this rebellion, but it claims to give us all the information we need to be completely equipped for this struggle.

Second Timothy 3:16,17 tells us that "all Scripture is God-breathed and profitable for teaching, for reproof, for correction, and for training in righteousness, that the man of God may be adequate, equipped for every good work." This passage gives us some valuable information about the Scriptures. First, it tells us that the source of the Bible is God. This is not a book written by men who are relating their religious experiences with God, but a book written *by God through men* to inform us about every area of life.

The apostle Peter makes this clear in 2 Peter 1:20: "Know this first of all, that no prophecy of Scripture is a matter of one's own interpretation." Peter is saying that the human authors of Scripture did not just reflect on their experiences of life, write them down, and call this the Word of God. That is the approach of men without revelation from God. Instead, Peter insists that it was the divine Author who initiated and produced God's Word: "No prophecy was ever made by an act of human will, but men moved by the Holy Spirit spoke from God" (2 Peter 1:21). The word usually translated "inspired" in 2 Timothy 3:16 is from the Greek word *theopneustos*, meaning "God breathed." The source of the Scriptures is the true God, who is not a liar. Therefore the Bible is absolutely true in everything it affirms.

Second, because the Bible is absolute truth, it is profitable to teach us, to correct our thinking, to reprove or reprimand us for wrong thinking and living, and to instruct us. Our Lord said in His prayer for the disciples the night before He was crucified, "Sanctify them in the truth; Thy word is truth" (John 17:17). It is *the Word of God alone* which gives us the truth we need to live for Him.

The third point we want to emphasize from 2 Timothy 3:16,17 is the purpose for the Word of God. It is to make the believer, the man or woman of God, completely equipped for every good work. The word translated "adequate" is the Greek word *artios*, which means "fit, complete, capable, sufficient." This means that the Word of God gives us the information or guidelines needed to meet every situation we face in life.

This is further emphasized by the word translated "fully equipped," which has the idea of being completely outfitted and prepared for every contingency. In the ancient world this word was used to describe a ship that was fully loaded for a voyage or a rescue boat that was completely outfitted and prepared for any emergency. The point is that the Bible claims not only to give us true and accurate information but *all* the information we need to handle *any and every* situation that might arise in our lives.

Enough for Every Need

This is not the only passage of Scripture which teaches this important doctrine that Scripture is completely and totally sufficient for every need in the Christian's life. In 2 Peter 1:3,4 we are told:

> His divine power has granted to us *everything* pertaining to life and godliness, through the true knowledge of Him who called us by His own glory and excellence. For by these He has granted to us His precious and magnificent promises, in order that *by them* you might become partakers of the divine nature, having escaped the corruption that is in the world by lust [emphasis added].

As we will describe in the next chapter, the corruption that is in the world by lust came into the world as a result of the fall of the angel Lucifer, and the consequent fall of the human race as a result of the sin of Adam in the Garden of Eden. This passage teaches us that the only way to escape this corruption is by means of God's "precious and magnificent promises," and that through these promises God has given us everything we need to know pertaining to life and godliness.

The importance of the all-sufficiency of Scripture can hardly be overemphasized. In some segments of Christianity today the inerrancy and infallibility of Scripture is being questioned. But we believe that even among those who affirm the inerrancy and infallibility of Scripture, many Christians deny this authority of Scripture in the way they apply (or fail to apply) Scripture to their daily lives. Many Christians do not seem to view the Bible as sufficient for every good work when we look at certain practices which they have built upon viewpoints found outside the Bible. This is especially true in the area of spiritual warfare.

In recent years there has been much sensationalist teaching on demons and exorcism. It has been popular to teach people to "bind" the demons, to "take dominion" over Satan, or to give people special instructions for dealing with so-called "territorial spirits." We need to ask if these are scriptural concepts to begin with, and if so, what do they mean? We must also search the Scriptures to see exactly what form spiritual warfare takes, and what Christians are to do when they do encounter demonic forces.

The two passages we mentioned earlier, 2 Timothy 3:16 and 2 Peter 1:3,4, teach clearly that in the Bible God has given us everything we need to know to handle any situation which may arise in our lives. At the very least this includes every aspect of the spiritual life.

Why Go to School?

Whenever we have taught this principle that the Scriptures are totally sufficient for every need and situation in the believer's life, someone inevitably asks why, if this is true, we should even go to school or pursue studies in any other area. If this were true, the reasoning goes, then civilization would be set back hundreds of years and none of the technical advances which have been made in the history of civilization would have taken place because all people would have done was study the Bible.

This question arises because people do not realize how the truth of God's Word impacts all the different realms of life. In this book we are talking about the sufficiency of God's Word in enabling us to live a life pleasing to God. God's Word does not claim to be a textbook about oceanography or accounting or engineering, though it does contain some broad information about these areas of study.

What the Bible claims to provide is *absolute truth in all areas of Christian life and spirituality*. At the very least this must include information about the spiritual realm and how it impacts Christians. The Bible claims to tell us the truth about life, our purpose for existence, and how we can lay hold of our eternal destiny. All of these are issues in spiritual warfare. Therefore spiritual warfare and the world of the demonic is one of those areas in which Christians should acknowledge the exclusive authority of the Bible.

This book will not be dealing with how a biblical philosophy of life (some call it "worldview") is derived from the Bible and applied to broader, extrabiblical areas of learning found in God's creation. In a nutshell, the Bible deals with every area of life indirectly through the grid or framework which is taken directly from the Bible. Within this biblical framework or mindset we can examine the underlying principles of science, art, literature, politics, recreation, etc., and evaluate them in the light of God's standards.

The Bible doesn't tell us exactly how to pass a test for our driver's license, but it *does* tell us that we should obey the government by having a driver's license if we drive a car. Also, it tells us that we should glorify God in everything we do, including the way in which we take the test for the driver's license. Therefore the Bible *does* speak to every area of life in God's world, either directly (as in the case of spiritual warfare) or indirectly (as in the case of getting a driver's license).

Reliance upon experience and reason when dealing with spiritual warfare principles is so common today that we need to evaluate the role that experience and reason should play in finding the truth about spiritual warfare. We must ask the same question that Pontius Pilate asked Jesus: "What is truth?" (John 18:38). The answer to this question will enable us to learn God's principles about spiritual warfare.

What Is Truth?

Simply put, truth is what God says it is. People can find truth in God's Word. Something is true or false in terms of how it squares with what God says about it, no matter what the majority of people think on a given Gallup Poll. Truth is not relative but absolute and universal. There is not one truth that is true for one person and an opposite truth that is true for someone else. If truth were relative, then there would be situations where principles would apply randomly to various people. For example, if two people jumped off a tall building, then one might go up toward the sky while the other would plunge down to the pavement: Instead, all people fall down, because truth is true for all people. You cannot beat Christ's clear and simple statement on this subject: "Thy word is truth" (John 17:17b).

Psalm 36:9 says, "With Thee is the foundation of life; in Thy light we see light." Psalm 119:130 declares, "The unfolding of Thy words gives light; it gives understanding to the simple." The Bible tells us that we come to know truth by God's gracious revelation of Himself. We can respond to His Word either by submitting to it and thinking God's own thoughts or by rebelling against His light and thinking our own thoughts. Therefore there are two basic approaches to our search for truth and knowledge. Either we are *dependent* upon God and the light of His revelation or else we are *independent* of God and attempt to discover truth by our own fallible thinking.

Finding the Truth

There may be two ways to *search* for truth, but there is only one way to *find* truth, and that is by taking God's word for it. In fact, since "the sum of Thy word is truth" (Psalm 119:160), to look for spiritual truth in any place other than God's Word is to guarantee that we will not find it. This point is driven home by Christ in His comments about the two ways to search for truth: "Everyone who comes to Me, and hears My words, and acts upon them... is like a man building a house, who dug deep and laid a foundation upon the rock" (Luke 6:47,48).

Christ is saying that stability in life starts with trust in His Word, and that we need to dig deep in order to lay a sure foundation upon the rock of God's Word. Many Christians are convinced that God's Word is true, but they do not dig deep into God's Word in order to build their lives upon God's bedrock of truth. The benefit of laying our foundation for life upon the rock is that "when a flood rose, the torrent burst against that house and could not shake it, because it had been well built" (verse 48b).

The believer who is truly grounded upon God's Word will not be wiped out by the flood of problems which we all face in life. Those who do not have confidence that God's Word is the rock will fail, along with those who have not taken the time or effort to dig down to the bedrock. Christ depicts "the one who has heard, and has not acted accordingly" to someone who "built a house upon the ground without any foundation; and the torrent burst against it and immediately it collapsed, and the ruin of that house was great" (verse 49).

The emphasis of Christ's contrast is between the one who dug down to the rock and built a proper foundation and the one who did not extend the effort to dig, but just built upon the ground without adequate preparation. Those who are not grounded upon the foundation of God's Word are not able to withstand the storms of life without suffering severe damage. When the spiritual battle heats up in their lives they fall apart and end up living as if still under Satan's control. Those founded upon the truth find God and His Word to be more than sufficient in handling the adversities of life. When the battle comes to them they are able to stand firm and are not tossed about by the winds of false doctrine (Ephesians 4:11-14).

Which Viewpoint?

There are only two basic ways of looking at things: God's way, which we will call the divine viewpoint, or man's way, which we will call the human viewpoint. From beginning to end the Bible expresses one consistent view of life and addresses every issue of life from that viewpoint—God's viewpoint on life. Understanding and applying God's viewpoint leads to life, but living according to the human viewpoint leads to death: "There is a way which seems right to a man, but its end is the way of death" (Proverbs 14:12; 16:25).

The divine viewpoint and the human viewpoint can be illustrated by the two basic approaches a parent can use when assembling a new toy for his child's Christmas present. One approach is to read the instructions and follow the steps given by the manufacturer who made the toy. If the instructions are clear, and the parent has read and understood the directions, then the parent can produce a toy that is properly assembled and ready for the child to play with. The person operating from the divine viewpoint diligently studies God's Word so he can look at life through God's eyes—His Word—and apply it to his own life. What satisfying results, when the directions are followed carefully!

The other approach is used when the parent either doesn't want to bother to read the instructions or doesn't want to acknowledge that he is dependent upon something or someone other than himself in order to do the project right. Sometimes we think we are familiar enough with a particular kind of toy that we can rely solely on our intuition or experience. This is similar to living on the basis of the human viewpoint about life and spiritual matters. No matter the cost, we think we must do it ourselves, without reading, understanding, and following the manufacturer's instructions. More often than not this approach results in a toy that doesn't work properly or a frustrated parent who cannot understand why the manufacturer included all those extra parts!

Independence and Idolatry

Independence and *idolatry* are the two main reasons for adopting the human viewpoint in our search for truth. Independence, characterized by self-assertion, self-rule, or self law, forms the foundation of idolatry. In the arena of knowledge, the independent person constructs a worldview based on his own limited experience and reason. This is what Adam and Eve did, and it resulted in their tragic sin. An independent or autonomous person has an attitude of inner hostility toward God's revelation and creation (Romans 3:10-12; 8:5-11). Since God has left His fingerprints upon virtually everything, it is not surprising to see rebellious humanity attempting to wipe off God's set of fingerprints and replace them with their own. This explains why unbelievers are often not even aware that they are rebelling against certain things.

While it is true that the person operating on the human viewpoint may include certain ideas from God's Word that are true (just as Satan did in the Garden), these ideas are always modified or interpreted to fit the person's self-determined framework. This can be compared to taking pieces from one jigsaw puzzle to fill the gaps left by missing pieces in another puzzle. The pieces may or may not fit exactly, but in their new place they have a different meaning because they are in a different context. As Paul said in Romans 1:25, the way of the human viewpoint is to exchange "the truth of God for a lie." Never will an independent thinker bow his knee to the full authority of God's Word.

Whenever the God of the Bible is removed from the picture, something else takes His place. This is what the Bible calls idolatry. As Romans 1:18-25 makes clear, when the Creator is not the object of worship, the only candidates left are found in the creation. Whether the object of worship is a physical idol, an idea, or a lifestyle, ultimately it is *man* being worshiped because man is the one who attempts to control the situation by determining what will be worshiped. *Idolatry is the worship of anything in place of the God of the Bible.* All gods other than the God of the Bible are simply projections of man's own self. The narcissism of contemporary America is a classic example of this self-worship.

Two Pursuits of Truth

Within the realm of the human viewpoint, there are usually two general ways that people attempt to establish truth. The first approach in attempting to find truth independent of God and His Word is often called *reason* or rationalism. In its pure form rationalism is the belief that each person is born with certain innate ideas. On the basis of these innate ideas man can use reason and logic alone to discover ultimate truth, claims the rationalist. The rationalist does not believe that he must be dependent upon God's Word in order to think true thoughts about reality. Since rationalists do not think they need God's Word to think accurately, they replace God's Word as the starting point with the arrogant assumption that their own logic and reason alone is sufficient for arriving at truth. What idolatry!

The divine viewpoint does not reject the use of reason or logic, since God gave us a logical mind to use, but it rejects the *independent* or autonomous use of reason and logic. The divine viewpoint uses reason and logic *dependently*, starting with God's revelation as a basis in order to think God's thoughts after Him. This is called *the dependent use of logic*: logic used under the authority of God's Word to maintain consistency of thought in accordance with God's Word. The all-knowing God has already told us through revelation what is true, and dependent logic seeks to apply this truth to every issue in life to see how it does or does not correspond with God's revelation. (A person would be illogical to start with error, or a mixture of truth and error, to try to end up with truth.) Only when you start with *pure truth* as a foundation can you arrive at the full truth in all its ramifications. The psalmist said, "In Thy light, O God, do I see light."

The Misuse of Logic

The human viewpoint, on the other hand, uses reason and logic as the ultimate authority to determine what is possible and what is not possible. Reason is used to determine what can and cannot be, and then these conclusions are imposed on the Bible. This is evident in the thinking of those who reject the Bible's accounts of the miraculous. Because they cannot explain miracles on the basis of their own reason when they read miraculous accounts in the Bible, they reject these accounts as superstitious explanations. A rationalist denies the possibility that demons could possess and influence people, if he accepts the existence of demons at all. Because he cannot arrive at the existence of demons on the basis of his own reason and logic, he rejects the unseen world entirely. He seeks to explain it instead in terms of some naturalistic, cause-effect theory, since this is the only world he personally knows (because he has rejected the witness of God's Word). This puts human reason in the position of ultimate authority: Human reason determines what is and is not true in God's Word. By putting reason at a higher level than the Bible, reason replaces God and so becomes an idol.

The real conflict is not between using reason at all and not using reason at all, but between *using reason under the authority of God* and *using reason independently of God*. The true issue is *the proper place and use of logic*. The human viewpoint uses logic in an idolatrous way, placing it in the arena reserved exclusively for God's Word.

The fatal flaw in this use of reason is that it provides *no external, objective criterion* for evaluating its conclusions (since it rejects the Bible as a valid criterion). Ultimately this position must lapse into some form of subjectivity such as mysticism or emotionalism, since reason alone can never establish an objective criterion upon which to determine why one thing is true and another is not.

The rationalist rejects the resurrection of Christ as irrational by asserting that his reason is so great and his knowledge so extensive that he knows for a fact that such a thing as resurrection could never have happened. This is not only arrogant but extremely subjective. God never intended people to use reason as a tool to establish what is ultimately true; this is the role of God's Word alone. Reason and logic were given as tools *to enable us to study God's Word and help us think consistently in terms of it* so that we may faithfully apply it in every area of our lives. We are stressing this point because it is crucially important to realize that reason and experience are miserable failures when it comes to providing sure knowledge about God, angels, the nature of man, the need for salvation, and the meaning of life. *Only the Bible provides the basis for such knowledge.* Ultimately the consistent rationalist must reject the existence of God, angels, and demons because he has no way of verifying their existence.

Misusing Experience

Since independent reason cannot serve as a basis for arriving at the truth about God, angels, man, salvation, and the meaning of life, philosophers have searched elsewhere for a solid rock on which to build their views. This second human-viewpoint approach to truth is often called *experience* or *empiricism*. This is the backbone of the scientific method. Empiricists believe that knowledge of ultimate truth can be arrived at on the basis of sense perceptions. They claim that through the use of observation, collecting facts, forming hypotheses, testing hypotheses, and further testing of sense data, man can ultimately arrive at true knowledge about the existence of God, angels, the nature of man, salvation, and the meaning of life.

While the empirical approach when used correctly does have a place within the plan of God, the human viewpoint once again misuses God's intended purpose for this ability. Through the use of empiricism in science people can make many important observations about God's creation. Empirical observations have helped propel great advances in industry and technology in the last two centuries. Yet without a framework which consistently interprets and applies the results of empirical observations, competing and contradictory systems of thought develop. Only the Word of God provides an adequate basis for consistently evaluating and applying the results of empiricism.

Ants and Angels

If we rely solely on empiricism apart from biblical revelation, we will not always draw accurate conclusions. A look at the work habits and social behavior of ants provides an interesting illustration. One observer would note that there are multiple mates for any one female. Another person might observe that the ants are industrious workers. Without the biblical framework, human-viewpoint thinkers could take both observations and apply them to human society. In fact some modern sociologists have done just that in observing the rarity of monogamy in the animal kingdom and suggesting that multiple mates would be a better situation in human life, thereby rejecting the biblical idea of one mate until death. In contrast to the subjectivity of this approach, the Bible gives us the framework for rightly applying the data discovered through observation. We are to learn from the ants in their diligence, but not in their mating habits (Proverbs 6:6-11).

This same principle applies in the area of the existence of angels and demons. The empiricist will gather all the information he can from those who claim to have had some experience with an angel or a demon, or those who have helped deliver people from demonic influence. He will find out what they learned from these encounters and which methods, in their opinion, proved successful in delivering a person from the demonic oppression. He will collect these case studies and then draw conclusions about what we are to do when we encounter a demon. Even when the Bible is consulted with this process, no matter how high the empiricist's view of Scripture, in practice the Bible is treated as just another voice or witness to demonic activity. This always results in adjusting the biblical teaching on demons until it fits with the conclusions of various experiences.

Adding to Scripture

There are numerous problems with the pure empirical method, but the fundamental problem is a rejection of the complete sufficiency of Scripture. Rather than believing that the Bible tells us everything we need to know about angels and demons, the empiricist seeks to find out more. Rather than being satisfied with what God has said on the subject, the empiricist bases his understanding of demons on experiences that he or other people have had. This ultimately leads to much speculation about demons: what they do, what they look like, what their names are, how to perform exorcisms, and how to protect ourselves from demons. We need to remember that the Bible expressly forbids such speculation because it goes beyond the information contained in the Scriptures (1 Corinthians 4:6; 1 Timothy 1:4; 2 Timothy 2:23).

One writer demonstrates this contemporary use of experience over Scripture in his treatment of spiritual warfare with territorial spirits. He suggests that even as it is a common practice to discover the names of specific demons in order to deliver an afflicted individual, "it might be reasonable to postulate that it could also be done with territorial spirits."[1] Experience is then relied upon in order to determine the names of territorial spirits:

> Another Latin American, Rita Cabezas, has done considerable research on the names of the highest levels of the hierarchy of Satan. I will not at this point describe her research methodology except to mention that the beginning stages were associated with her extensive psychological/deliverance practice and that it later evolved into receiving revelatory words of knowledge. She has discovered that directly under Satan are six worldwide principalities, named (allowing that this was done in Spanish) Damian, Asmodeo, Menguelesh, Arios, Beelzebub and Nosferasteus. Under each, she reports, are six governors over each nation. For example, those over Costa Rica are Shiebo, Quiebo, Ameneo, Mephistopheles, Nostradamus and Azazel. Those over the U.S.A. are Ralphes, Anoritho, Manchester, Apolion, Deviltook, and one unnamed.[2]

1. C. Peter Wagner and F. Douglas Pennoger, eds., *Wrestling with Dark Angels* (Ventura, CA: Regal Books, 1990), pp. 84-5.
2. Ibid., p. 85.

Like any good empiricist, this writer does not fully rely upon this information alone, but seeks verification. But verification is only circumstantially found in the Bible. Considered as having equal validity with the Bible are the *Dictionary of Gods and Goddesses, Devils, and Demons*, the Apocrypha, *Paradise Lost*, and *Pilgrim's Progress* (which are the other sources used to validate the above statement). The whole statement is treated as having credibility simply because two of the names happen to have been mentioned in the Bible.

Borderline Spiritism

Also invalid because the demons could manipulate the data.

This type of activity comes dangerously close to spiritism, in which information gained either directly or indirectly from demonic encounters is made a part of teaching on demons. In the same paper on territorial spirits the author accepts as valid the information received from a former occult leader regarding the number of demons and their operations in Nigeria.[3] This information was gained while he was an occult leader, and so its source is demonic. We must remember that Satan is a liar and a deceiver. Methods that he and the demons use are often designed to confuse and distract Christians by getting them involved in illegitimate areas, with the result that they unwittingly end up serving Satan's ends rather than God's.

An extreme example of this occurred in the mid-seventies. A man by the name of John Todd found wide acceptance in certain Christian circles by giving people "inside information" about Satan and his current schemes (which he had had access to as a former Satanist). Todd's teachings included such information as the proper names of some of the demons, how they are organized, and certain of their strategies and tactics. None of this information was gleaned from the Bible; rather, it was gained from the time Todd spent as a Satanist (which he relied upon even as a believer). Many people within Christian circles were eager to listen to this information gleaned from demons, until they learned that Todd had fabricated much of what he was saying, while at the same time seducing young Christian girls into immorality.

Deceptions and Discrepancies

We are so limited in our ability to truly discern what is taking place in the spirit realm that we are often completely distracted and in some

3. Ibid., p. 76.

cases downright duped. Several years ago an associate of ours whom we will call Bill was involved in counseling a woman whose background was marked by years of sexual abuse. From early childhood she had been raped and sexually abused by her father. In her twenties she heard the gospel and put her faith in Jesus Christ as her Savior. Though saved, she still struggled with many issues which were rooted in her past. During the time Bill was counseling with her, he discussed her case with a pastor from Fort Worth. This pastor suggested that the reason this girl had never had victory over these past problems was because of demonic influence or possession. He believed that demons were involved in every case of sexual abuse, and suggested an exorcism.

One night Bill and the woman met with three pastors in Fort Worth for an exorcism. They apparently contacted seven different demons, which they then cast out of her. She went home much relieved. However, her "healing" had only short-term results, for she still had problems.

Several months later Bill discovered a series of discrepancies in the woman's account of her life, and began to question if there had ever been any sexual abuse in the first place. He and another man who had counseled her then confronted her with the evidence, and she admitted that most of what she had said and done was made up. When they asked her about the exorcism episode, she finally admitted that it had all been an act motivated by her confusion and what she perceived the expectations of her counselors to be.

Since then we have discovered that this woman has had a long history of using her problems as a means of gaining attention and care from other Christians. She has gone from church to church and group to group over a period of several years with the sad story of her life. Each time some concerned and caring Christians have taken her in and helped her. However, each time they would discover her deception, and then she would drop out of sight temporarily, only to surface again at another church. At this time she is under the care of a nationally known biblical counselor. According to him she was never demon-possessed or demon-influenced in the first place, and the whole episode only served to complicate an already-complex spiritual problem.

The Failure of Secular Systems

The point of this story is to show that two groups of people who claim to be biblical attempted to help an unfortunate woman. In one case the solution was sought through a demonic deliverance, and in another case the solution was sought through the use of Scripture in counseling. We are not attempting here to decide whether this girl was ever demonized; the point we are making is that one particular group of pastors, who had had years of experience in a deliverance ministry and had developed a technique of dealing with demonized people based on experience, were apparently fooled. (If they were not, then their empirically developed deliverance techniques were a failure.) Anytime we base a technique for dealing with demonized people on anything other than the clear teaching of the Word of God, we are doomed to failure. In fact, using any approach based on information not directly derived from the Scriptures is in practice a denial of the authority and sufficiency of the Bible. These examples simply show the inadequacy of personal experience in validating demon-possession.

In the last two centuries many philosophical systems have sought to combine rationalism and empiricism. However, if neither of these two methods can arrive at certainty about God and the spiritual realm on their own, combining them will not solve the problem either. Rationalism and empiricism both fail to provide an adequate basis for objectively verifying knowledge about the spiritual realm. How then *can* we know about the existence of God and angels and about the nature of man, salvation, and the meaning of life?

The Only True Basis

The only trustworthy basis for knowledge about the supernatural is God's revelation. Since man is incapable of arriving at ultimate truth through his own resources, whether through reason or sense data, he must rely upon God's revelation. In Romans 1 Paul tells us that while human beings have a clear testimony of God in the creation all around them, they reject that evidence because they are sinners: "That which is known about God is evident within them, for God made it evident to them. For since the creation of the world His invisible attributes, His eternal power and divine nature, have been clearly seen, being understood through what has been made, so that they are without excuse. For even though they knew God, they did not honor Him as God, or give thanks; but they became futile in their speculations, and their foolish heart was darkened" (Romans 1:19-21).

The effect of Adam's sin on the abilities of the human mind is extensive, and must never be underestimated when discussing the issue of knowing truth. The above passage from Romans 1 tells us that man's heart is darkened. In Romans 3:11,12 we are told, "There is none who understands; there is none who seeks for God. All have turned aside, together they have become useless; there is none who does good, there is not even one." Paul again stresses the effects of sin in Romans 8:7,8: "The mind set on the flesh [the mind of the unsaved person] is hostile toward God; for it does not subject itself to the law of God, for it is not even able to do so; and those who are in the flesh cannot please God."

God describes the effect of sin on man in a number of different ways: He says that the unsaved are in darkness, that Satan works within them, that they are blind and ignorant, that they willfully suppress the truth, and that they are enslaved to sin and unrighteousness. The only path out of this predicament is the Word of God.

The Only Deliverer

In the eighth chapter of the Gospel of John we are told of a very important dialogue between Jesus and some of the Jewish leaders. In that interchange He said, "You shall know the truth, and the truth shall make you free" (verse 32). It is *the Word of God* that brings light into darkness and tells us everything we need to know about sin and Satan, and how to be set free from them. Remember Psalm 119:130, which we noted earlier: "The unfolding of Thy words gives light; it gives understanding to the simple."

Some Pharisees who were in the crowd objected to Christ's statement, claiming that since they were Abraham's offspring they were not in need of being liberated. But in fact they were enslaved in at least four ways: They were in bondage to the Roman Empire, they were in bondage to the traditions of the Pharisees, they were in bondage to Satan, and they were in bondage to sin. Jesus stated that the only means of freedom was through Him: "If therefore the Son shall make you free, you shall be free indeed" (John 8:36).

The only source of deliverance from bondage is Jesus Christ. According to Colossians 1:13, all people are born in the domain of darkness. But through faith in Jesus Christ we are delivered from the domain of darkness and transferred to the kingdom of Jesus Christ. If you have never taken the opportunity to trust Christ as your Savior, you too are enslaved to sin and Satan, and the only way you can be free is to trust in Jesus Christ as your Savior.

The Equipment You Need

We hope you have seen that as God's creatures we are dependent upon His Word alone as the sole basis for evaluating our thoughts and experiences in relationship to everything, but especially those things which He has dealt with specifically, such as God, angels, demons, the nature of man, the need for salvation, and the meaning of life. While most Christians agree in theory that God's Word is sufficient to deal with the issues of Christian living, more and more Christians are denying the sufficiency of God's Word in daily practice. Rather than relying on the Bible alone, they seek more information about Satan and demons and end up relying upon information gained from former occult leaders and from various experiences with demons. This information is then taught to Christians as biblical doctrine when in fact its source is demonic (read 1 Timothy 4:1).

In the chapters to come we will show that God's Word alone is sufficient to equip you for a holy rebellion against the devil, the world, and the flesh.

– 3 –

ORIGINS OF CONFLICT

You said in your heart, "I will ascend to heaven; I will raise my throne above the stars of God, and I will sit on the mount of assembly in the recesses of the north. I will ascend above the heights of the clouds; I will make myself like the Most High."

—Isaiah 14:13,14

Just a short look at the newspaper or the evening news lets us know that evil is a very real problem in this world. Child abuse, murder, rape, terrorism, and divorce all reveal to us that life is not what it ought to be. All people seem to have this awareness. Not only is life different from what it ought to be in the lives of human beings, but natural disasters such as floods, hurricanes, tornadoes, and earthquakes all testify that even in the realm of nature things are not what they ought to be. How did things get so messed up? Is this just the way it happens to be, or is there something more to it?

Four Answers

When confronted with the existence of evil there are only four possible responses. Over the centuries people have suggested three ways of resolving the problem of evil apart from the Scriptures. The first is to deny evil. This is reflected in the thinking of the Greek philosophy called Platonism, some Eastern religions, and most mind-science religions (such as Christian Science). Sometimes these systems of thought claim to be dualistic and recognize some form of evil, but since ultimate reality for them is "one," if consistent they must deny the ultimate existence of real evil. According to this view what we encounter in everyday life is simply an illusion; it is not real. Pain and suffering are merely illusions; ultimate reality exists on a higher plane.

A second way of resolving the problem of evil is to deny morality. This view denies the sense of a moral "ought." Evil is a natural part of reality. If you accept the conclusions of scientific evolution, then there is no basis for morality, no basis for distinguishing between good and evil. T.H. Huxley, noted evolutionist, clearly recognized this principle:

> The thief and murderer follow nature just as much as the philanthropist. Cosmic evolution may teach us how the good and evil tendencies of man may have come about: but, in itself, it is incompetent to furnish any better reason why what we call good is preferable to what we call evil than we had before.[1]

A third way that people have sought to resolve the problem of evil is to simply resign themselves to accept this tension as part of the absurdity of life. This is the answer of modern existentialism, which says that life is basically absurd, that there are no rational explanations—so just enjoy your life. Frank Sinatra's popular song "That's Life" embodies this approach. He sings, "You're riding high in April, shot down in May." The rest of the song conveys the idea that you just have to learn to roll with the punches, because that's life and there's really nothing you can do about the nature of it.

In contrast to these attempts to resolve the problem of evil on the basis of the independent use of human reason and experience, the Bible clearly teaches that evil is neither an illusion nor natural. God's original creation was holy and perfect and devoid of evil. Evil in the universe is the direct consequence of the sin of the creature Lucifer. It was this sin, this act of rebellion on the part of the creature, which began the angelic rebellion against God, the great war in the heavenly realm. It is in this great war that the human race is involved. The only way we can know about this is through God's revelation in the Bible.

How the War Began

Before we can begin to understand how we are involved in this war, why we are involved, and what we should do about it, we must first understand how the war began. The Bible clearly reveals Lucifer's attempt to establish his own rebel kingdom in defiance of God. From the biblical account of this takeover plot we learn of Lucifer's goals

1. Quoted by Cyril Bibbly in *T.H. Huxley* (New York: Horizon Press, 1960), p. 84.

and strategies, his abilities, how he subverted the human race and brought them under his authority and kingdom, and how God provided a way for the human race to renounce their allegiance to this evil ruler. By turning to God we are rebelling against the unholiness and evil of Satan and his kingdom. This is the beginning of our holy rebellion.

The Bible tells us that Satan is the prince of darkness, the "ruler of this world" and the "god of this age." During this present time God has allowed Satan to have his own realm, domain, or kingdom, and Satan's kingdom of darkness is at war against the kingdom of light. Light and darkness are often used in the Bible as figures of speech for God's kingdom (light in 1 Timothy 6:16 and 1 John 1:5,7) and Satan's kingdom (darkness in Luke 22:53; Ephesians 5:8; 6:12; 1 Peter 2:9). Satan is the one against whom Christians are in rebellion. Scripture clearly teaches that everyone is born in Satan's "domain of darkness" (Colossians 1:13; cf. Acts 26:18). The original Greek word for "domain" means *authority*. When we are born we are under the authority of Satan, who is the god of this world (2 Corinthians 4:4), yet when we turn to God at the point of salvation by trusting in Jesus Christ as our Savior, this same verse says that we are transferred to the kingdom of His beloved Son. The allegiance of the Christian is now given to God rather than Satan. Christians have become holy rebels against the god of this age. If we are going to be effective as rebels, we must understand exactly what the Bible teaches about Satan, how he became Satan, and what his goal is for planet Earth.

The Sons of God

The first beings that God created to inhabit His kingdom were an order of spirit beings called angels. In one of the oldest books of the Bible, Job, we are told of a man named Job who faced an incredible number of personal tragedies. After holding out for awhile he finally began to question the goodness and judgment of God. In Job 38:4-7 God replied by turning Job's attention to his own limitations and to God's work of creation:

> Where were you when I laid the foundation of
>   the earth!
> Tell Me, if you have understanding,
> Who set its measurements, since you know?
> Or who stretched the line on it?

On what were its bases sunk?
Or who laid its cornerstone,
When the morning stars sang together,
And all the sons of God shouted for joy?

At the time of the creation of the earth all the angels were still unified. The term "sons of God" is an expression used in the Old Testament to refer to angels. There was no hint of division or rebellion, no pride, no one trying to outdo anyone else. They *all* rejoiced together over God's new creation!

The Highest of the Angels

However, this unity did not continue. At some point a tragic split occurred among the angelic host. The highest of all the angels, Lucifer, decided that he wanted to be like God. When God removed this rebellious angel from his position of authority, Lucifer gathered a group of other angels and led them in a revolt against God. The two passages in Scripture which describe these events also reveal critical information about Lucifer/Satan which we must know in order to understand our enemy and to avoid falling into his traps, because there is no indication anywhere in the Scripture that he has changed since that day of rebellion.

The description of Lucifer is found in Ezekiel 28:11-19. At the beginning of this chapter Ezekiel is instructed to take up a lament against the prince or leader of the city of Tyre. In the first ten verses Ezekiel pronounces judgment upon the prince of Tyre because he has said in his heart that he is a god. In verses 11-19 a second lament is taken up, but here it is directed not to the *prince* of Tyre but to the *king* of Tyre. The things said of this king of Tyre could not possibly apply to the human leader of Tyre. For example, he is said to have existed in Eden, the garden of God (verse 13) and to have been created blameless (verse 15). It seems that the person addressed in this section is the real power behind the human king of Tyre: Satan or Lucifer. Often in Scripture Satan is addressed through the creature he is influencing. For example, when Jesus foretold His crucifixion, Peter began to rebuke Him. But Jesus rebuked Peter and said, "Get behind Me, Satan!" (Matthew 16:23). In addition, when God pronounced a curse on Satan in Genesis 3:14,15 He addressed Satan indirectly through the serpent. So the "king of Tyre" mentioned here is none other than Satan himself.

Here is how Ezekiel describes Lucifer in 28:12-16:

> Take up a lamentation over the king of Tyre, and say to him, "Thus says the Lord God, 'You had the seal of perfection, full of wisdom and perfect in beauty. You were in Eden, the garden of God; every precious stone was your covering: the ruby, the topaz, and the diamond; the beryl, the onyx, and the jaspar; the lapis lazuli, the turquoise, and the emerald; and the gold, the workmanship of your settings and sockets, was in you. On the day that you were created they were prepared. You were the anointed cherub who covers, and I placed you there. You were on the holy mountain of God; you walked in the midst of the stones of fire. You were blameless in your ways from the day you were created, until unrighteousness was found in you. By the abundance of your trade you were internally filled with violence, and you sinned; therefore I have cast you as profane from the mountain of God. And I have destroyed you, O covering cherub, from the midst of the stones of fire.' "

Here we see Satan in all his pre-fall perfection and glory. All these descriptions clearly indicate that Lucifer was the greatest of all the angels in every way.

Model of Perfection

He was created as *the model or prototype of perfection.* He is described as "having the seal of perfection," which in the Hebrew language has the idea of one who sets the standard. Just as the ultimate national standard for all measurement is in the National Bureau of Standards, so Lucifer was the ultimate standard of perfection. This clearly shows his superiority over all other creatures. Later, in verse 15, we are told that he was blameless, or perfect, in all his ways.

As the prototype or pattern of perfection he was also the most beautiful and glorious of the angels. He was "full of beauty." His appearance was nothing less than magnificent, and this was further enhanced by his dress. His personal adornment was splendid and indicated a very high position. He was covered with a brilliant collection of precious stones. Whenever these jewels are mentioned together in Scripture they have something to do with the very presence of God. Eight of the nine jewels were in the breastplate worn by the high priest of Israel (Exodus 28:17-20) and six are also found in the foundation stones of the wall of the New Jerusalem (Revelation 21:19,20).

Another way Lucifer was the standard of perfection was in his intelligence, for he was "full of wisdom." Wisdom in the Bible is not simply great knowledge but the ability to skillfully apply that knowledge. Lucifer was the most intelligent and the most beautiful creature made by God.

Not only did he have looks and brains, but he also had power and authority to go with these. He was "the anointed cherub." The word "anointed" means "one who is set apart to God for a special task." This is the same word that is transliterated Messiah, and is rendered in English by the word "Christ" in the New Testament. Lucifer is the first creature ever designated as "the anointed one." In Scripture three groups of people were anointed: prophets, priests, and kings. Prophets speak God's word to people, priests carry the worship of the people to God, and kings rule over subjects. Before he sinned, Lucifer functioned as a prophet, priest, and king. He was the ruler of the angels and led them in their worship and praise of God.

An Anointed Cherub

Lucifer was also a cherub, one of the highest ranks of angels associated with the glory and presence of God. When God instructed Moses to build the ark of the covenant, He told him to place two cherubs on top of it looking down on the mercy seat (Exodus 37:9). Their wings were to *cover* the mercy seat, and this is the same word for covering that is used here in Ezekiel 28:13,14. Typically the image that comes to mind when people hear cherubs mentioned is that of a baby with wings. This absurd notion has no basis at all in Scripture, but was the innovation of medieval artists. Scripture has a completely different description of cherubs:

> This was their appearance: they had human form. Each of them had four faces and four wings. And their legs were straight and their feet were like a calf's hoof, and they gleamed like burnished bronze. Under their wings on their four sides were human hands. As for the faces and wings of the four of them, their wings touched one another. Their faces did not turn when they moved; each went straight forward. As for the form of their faces, each had the face of a man, all four had the face of a lion on the right and the face

of a bull on the left, and all four had the face of an eagle (Ezekiel 1:5-10).

Cherubs were also embroidered on the veil or screen which separated the innermost room of the tabernacle, the holy of holies, from the outer room, the holy place. They were earthly symbols of God's heavenly throne room. The word for "veil" is the same word translated "covering." Apparently Lucifer's position in the throne room of God involved personally covering the throne of God with his wings. He held a very exalted position indeed!

That Lucifer operated in the very presence of God is further emphasized by the statements that he was in "Eden, the garden of God," which could refer to the earthly Garden of Eden but more likely refers to the heavenly throne of God, since he was "on the holy mountain of God" and "walked in the midst of the stones of fire" (a phrase used of God's presence).

As far as a creature can be said to be perfect, this one was. His appearance was so impressive and brilliant that Isaiah referred to him as "Lucifer" (14:12 KJV), which means "lightbearer" and was a reference to the morning star, the planet Venus, which announced the coming of the sun by its reflection of the sun's light. In the same way Satan appears to have been the herald of God through his reflections of God's glory.

Turning Point

Verse 15 describes the turning point in the life of this creature. It clearly states that he had been created blameless. God did not originate evil; evil originated in the heart of the creature. The reason is given in the next verse: "By the abundance of your trade you were internally filled with violence, and you sinned." If we read between the lines a little, there seems to be an analogy here between the reason for Lucifer's sin and what was going on in Tyre. Tyre was a maritime power whose economy was built upon trade. Because the people of Tyre excelled greatly and had a trade balance that put them in a position of power over other nations, they sought to take advantage of this fact to build their own kingdom. Apparently part of Lucifer's responsibility was to carry the worship of the angelic hosts to God in his priestly function, and in so doing he began to trade on his influence to build his own kingdom. When Lucifer sinned, Satan's career began. The exact nature of this sin is further described by Isaiah.

Isaiah is told to "take up this taunt against the king of Babylon" (Isaiah 14:4). A "taunt" was a discourse designed to humble those who have rebelled against God. As in the Ezekiel passage, the taunt is directed against a human king but the statements go far beyond the sin of any human king.

> How you have fallen from heaven, O star of the morning, son of the dawn! You have been cut down to the earth, you who have weakened the nations! But you said in your heart, "I will ascend to heaven; I will raise my throne above the stars of God, and I will sit on the mount of assembly in the recesses of the north. I will ascend above the heights of the clouds; I will make myself like the Most High." Nevertheless you will be thrust down to Sheol, to the recesses of the pit (Isaiah 14:12-15).

Sin began not with an external act but with the internal decision of the heart. Five times Satan said in his heart, "I will . . ." These statements show the essence of sin: The assertion of the creature's right to self-determination, independence from God, or personal autonomy. This is why the autonomous or independent use of reason, experience, or anything else is an expression of rebellion against God.

The Ultimate in Self-Esteem

Lucifer became so impressed with his own beauty, brilliance, intelligence, power, and position that he began to desire for himself the honor and glory that belonged to God alone. No creature ever felt better about himself or had a better self-image than Satan. He was no longer satisfied with obeying God, but instead wanted to overthrow God and be God himself. Filled with the violence of rebellion, he rejected the authority of God in his life, ignored the fact that he was who he was only because God made him that way, and led a revolt against God. The result was judgment. He was cast away as profane (Ezekiel 28:16). Profane is the opposite of holy; Lucifer became unholy because of his rebellion.

Lucifer's fall was the result of his decision to strive after self-exaltation, to assert his own position rather than to remain in a position of service to God. In other words, he gave in to arrogance and pride. (Christians are constantly reminded in the New Testament to avoid pride. First Peter 5:5 tells us that God is opposed to the proud.)

When Lucifer sinned, he did not sin alone, but led a massive angelic revolt against God. As he carried out his commerce among the angels he began to entice and seduce a number of them to serve him rather than God. When he sinned and was judged by God, these angels followed him and his unholy rebellion was launched. Scripture indicates that about a third of the angels followed him in his rebellion (Revelation 12:4).

These fallen or unholy angels are referred to in the Scripture as demons, evil spirits, or unclean spirits. They are angels who have rebelled against God. (Some have taught that they are the spirits of a pre-Adamic race or the souls of the wicked who have died, but there is no basis in Scripture for this opinion.)

What's in a Name?

Throughout the Scriptures we find that the names and titles given to people indicate something about their character. For example, Isaiah 9:6 records a prophecy about Jesus Christ which gives us four titles that tell us something about His character: "His name will be called Wonderful Counselor, Mighty God, Eternal Father, Prince of Peace." These names tell us about the character of the Messiah. *Wonderful Counselor* refers to the Messiah who will bring counsel for eternal life, and who will rule with perfect wisdom (Isaiah 11:2). *Mighty God* identifies Him with the power of God which will ultimately be victorious over evil. *Eternal Father* indicates both His eternal nature and His care for His people. *Prince of Peace* indicates that He is the one who brings peace, both personal and worldwide.

Just as we learn many important things about the Lord Jesus Christ from the titles and names given to Him, so we also learn much about Satan from the titles and names given to him. It is important for us to look at these so that we can accurately understand what he can do and his role in this age.

Serpent, dragon. In the Garden of Eden a serpent appeared to Eve and tempted her to disobey the command of God. In Genesis 3:1 we are told that "the serpent was more crafty than any beast of the field which the Lord God had made." The identity of this serpent is made clear in Revelation 12:9: "The great dragon was thrown down, the serpent of old who is called the devil and Satan, who deceives the whole world. . . ." This certainly tells us something about his character. In the creation account of man in Genesis 1:26, God made man to rule *over* the birds and *over* the cattle and *over* all the earth and *over* every creeping thing. Man was to rule *over* the serpent, yet the serpent was crafty enough to subvert this authority by getting man to listen and submit to him. We must remember that Satan was created full of wisdom. His guile and cunning is so great that he is able to confuse and deceive man to do his bidding if man does not trust in God's Word.

Satan, Devil, accuser of the brethren. Our word "devil" comes from the Greek word *diabolos*, which means "slanderer" or "accuser." In Revelation 12:10 Satan is called "the accuser of our brethren." A slanderer is one who makes false charges or lies which are intended to defame and to damage someone's reputation. *Satan* is from the Hebrew word which means "adversary" or "opponent." Satan opposes God's people in two ways. First, he brings charges against believers before God (Zechariah 3:1; Romans 8:33). Second, he accuses believers to their own conscience. His goal is to make us focus on our sin and guilt and to get us wrapped up in our attempts to deal with it on our own. Then we will forget that for the Christian sin is no longer the issue, since even though Satan has more than sufficient grounds to accuse believers, God looks upon us as righteous because of the righteousness of Christ which has been given to us.

Accused But Forgiven

A beautiful illustration of how God responds to Satan's accusations is found in Zechariah 3:1-5. There Zechariah had a vision of the heavenly courtroom scene. God is the Judge, and Joshua the High Priest of Israel is standing before God. Satan is present as the witness for the prosecution. The response of the Lord is to rebuke Satan as he indicts Joshua. The Lord reminds the court that Joshua has been "plucked out of the fire." Joshua, like all sinners, stands before God dressed in the filthy clothes of his sin. But God in His grace has clothed Joshua with clean garments of righteousness and a clean turban about his head. As a recipient of God's grace he is free from guilt and should no longer be troubled by Satan's accusations.

What a marvelous picture of what God does for every believer in the Lord Jesus Christ! Satan stands as our accuser. From one perspective he has every right to do this, for like Joshua we stand before God dressed in the filthy garments of our sin. Isaiah 64:6 says that "all our righteous deeds are like a filthy garment." However, when we trust in Jesus Christ, God graciously dresses us in His righteousness, so that we are no longer guilty and Satan has no ground to accuse us. This is the message of 1 John 1:1–2:2, which tells us that believers are continually cleansed by the blood of Jesus Christ. God cleanses, forgives, and justifies us, and Jesus Christ is our Defense Counsel, our Advocate with the Father.

If you are not a Christian, this means that no matter what you have done you can obtain complete forgiveness of sin by trusting in Jesus Christ. If you are a Christian, this means that when Satan seeks to accuse you, planting doubts in your mind because you have sinned or rebelled against God, you can stand firm on God's promise that you have been clothed with the righteousness of Christ and that for His sake God has forgiven you. There is then no need to cave in to guilt or to a defeatist mentality, and to do so is a denial of God's promise that He cleanses us and forgives us of all unrighteousness (1 John 1:9). Instead, we should be freely pursuing godliness and holiness in our lives.

More Sinister Names

The ruler of this world. Twice the Lord Jesus Christ refers to Satan in this way (John 12:31; 14:30). The word "world" here is translated from the Greek word *kosmos*, which encompasses the entire world system, including all the ideas and philosophies which Satan is promoting among people to establish his kingdom on the earth. Some of the more popular of these ideas today are secular humanism, evolution, psychology, materialism, Marxism, and the New Age movement.

We will say more about this in the next chapter, but here we want to remind every Christian that Satan is the ruler of this world, that we were born under his authority (compare Acts 26:18 with Colossians 1:13), and that when we believed in Jesus Christ as our Savior and Redeemer we committed the unforgivable sin as far as Satan is concerned. We declared our allegiance to the King of Kings and Lord of Lords and became rebels against Satan's illegitimate authority. He is now out to get us, and the only way we can successfully survive is by following the explicit instructions of Scripture.

Prince of the power of the air. This title is given to Satan in Ephesians 2:2. It is related to the title "ruler of this world" and refers to the atmosphere. Within God's permission, Satan has control of man's environment. This verse also points out that he is the spirit who is now working in the "sons of disobedience"—the unbelievers. Unbelievers are born under the authority of Satan as the ruler of this world, are influenced by him because he is the controller of the environment, and have Satan working in and through them.

God of this age. This title is closely tied to the two previous ones, and is found in 2 Corinthians 4:4. It is during this age, between the fall of Adam and Eve and the coming of Christ, that Satan has been given the freedom by God to propagate his worldly system. This verse goes on to say that he is blinding the unsaved to the truth. One reason that unbelievers do not understand the truth of the gospel message is that they are being blinded by Satan. The only way this is overcome is through the ministry of the Holy Spirit, who enlightens people to the truth.

Evil one. Satan is referred to by this title in several passages (Matthew 6:13; John 17:15; 2 Thessalonians 3:3; 1 John 5:19). In these verses we learn that in spite of his beauty, intelligence, and power, Satan is evil. Often his evil is a beautiful evil and not merely an ugly one, as is often thought. His evil pervades the whole world because it all lies in his power. Yet as rebels against this incredibly evil personage we have the protection of the Lord Jesus Christ. Christ in His present role as our intercessor prays that we be kept from the evil one. We are also promised that because of His faithfulness we will be strengthened and protected from the evil one (2 Thessalonians 3:3).

Tempter. This title is given of Satan in Matthew 4:3, when the Lord Jesus was led by the Holy Spirit into the wilderness to be tempted by the devil. This is what is called *objective* temptation. Satan entices and lures people to do his will. He sets the trap and baits it well, but he does not have the power to make anyone step into it. We can only fall prey to his temptation when we choose to do so. The reason we choose to but Jesus didn't is because we allow our sin nature to control us, and we fall into Satan's trap. The internal or *subjective* side of temptation is described in James 1:14: "Each one is tempted when he is carried away and enticed by his own lust." If we are to avoid the traps and spot the bait, we must do what Scripture says in order to control our sinful nature. (This will be discussed in a later chapter.)

Roaring lion. First Peter 5:8 warns every Christian to be of sober spirit, which means to have the right mindset: not to be distracted, but to be constantly alert because "your adversary, the devil, prowls about like a roaring lion, seeking someone to devour." This passage also gives us the advice we need in order to avoid these attacks. (These too will be further discussed in a later chapter.)

Deceiver. Paul referred to the deceptiveness of Satan and warned the Corinthians about it in 2 Corinthians 11:3. If Eve, who did not have a sin nature, was deceived by the craftiness of Satan, how much easier it is for believers who *do* have a sin nature! This deception can take any number of forms, but one form that Paul refers to in this chapter is *religious deception.* He warns us that in his role as deceiver Satan disguises himself as an "angel of light" and as a "servant of righteousness" (2 Corinthians 11:14,15). Satan has the power to deceive even through miracles and signs and wonders. In fact, this is the very tool he will use to deceive many people into following the coming Antichrist (2 Thessalonians 2:9-12). Jesus also warned that many who appear to be Christians and who even healed people, cast out demons, and performed many miracles *in His name* will be told by Him at the last judgment to depart because He never knew them (Matthew 7:21-23). The only way Christians can avoid the subtle deception of Satan is through a detailed knowledge of God's Word.

This picture which Scripture paints of Satan should cause every one of us to recognize the incredible danger that Satan presents to every human being. We must not forget who he is or how much power and intelligence he has. It is a serious mistake to become arrogant toward Satan and ridicule him, an attitude which is never reflected in the Scriptures. This type of mentality among Christians was reflected in the message seen recently on a signboard outside a church in the Midwest: "Jesus is Hefty, Hefty, Hefty; Satan is Wimpy, Wimpy, Wimpy."

Subversion of the Race

Satan's genius for being able to tailor a temptation to appeal to the individual is first seen in his attack on man in the Garden of Eden. Now that Satan had begun his rebellious kingdom, he wanted to extend its influence. In the Garden of Eden he was able to subvert mankind and bring them under his authority and dominion. As we look at how he did this, we see a basic pattern of attack which he commonly uses even today.

The crowning achievement of God's creation was mankind. This creative act took place on the sixth day, as recorded in Genesis 1:26,27:

> God said, "Let Us make man in Our image, according to Our likeness; and let them rule over the fish of the sea and over the birds of the sky and over the cattle and over all the earth, and over every creeping thing that creeps on the earth." And God created man in His own image, in the image of God He created him; male and female He created them.

God created the human race, one man and one woman, and placed them over the earth to rule it as His representatives.

As God's vice-regents over the planet, Adam and Eve were given everything they would need to carry out their responsibilities. (This is always true of God's gracious provision for His people.) God created the world and its environment in a perfect condition for man, then filled it with both animals and plants. He provided abundantly for the sustenance of man, and then instructed him about this provision (Genesis 1:29,30). And His continued presence gave Adam and Eve the opportunity to get answers to any problem they may have faced. God always provides everything man needs to fulfill his obligations to Him.

While God had provided everything for them, He also established one simple test by which Adam and Eve could demonstrate their love and devotion to Him: They were forbidden to eat of the fruit of one particular tree in the Garden. This tree was called the "tree of the knowledge of good and evil" (Genesis 2:17). The Hebrew word used for knowledge here means *experiential knowledge* rather than academic knowledge. We have no idea what kind of tree this was or what kind of fruit it bore. But the issue was made clear to both Adam and Eve: "From any tree of the garden you may eat freely; but from the tree of knowledge of good and evil you shall not eat, for in the day that you eat from it you shall surely die" (Genesis 2:16,17). The test was simple: If they loved and trusted God they would obey Him; if they did not, they would disobey Him and the result would be death.

Satan's Age-Old Strategy

After observing Adam and Eve, Satan apparently decided that if he could win Eve to his side it would be easier to win Adam. A careful analysis of Satan's approach to Eve reveals much that is characteristic of Satan's strategy even today. He began by disguising himself (in this case as a serpent). Genesis 3:1 states, "The serpent was more crafty than any beast of the field which the Lord God had made." Actually the word translated "crafty" here carries the idea of *malevolent brilliance*. Satan is in the business of deception. He does not appear openly, nor does he make his desires plain. Instead, he wraps them in the cloak of apparent good (2 Corinthians 11:14). Satan does not normally come up to people and say, "Do you want to sin?" Instead, his temptation usually takes the form of doing good.

Satan began to work on Eve by first questioning what God had said (Genesis 3:1). It is Satan's usual technique to cause people to first question the sufficiency of God and His Word and then question the truth of what God has revealed. God revealed to Adam and Eve that they were not to eat of the fruit from the tree of the knowledge of good and evil. He did not go into detail; He did not enlighten them about His reasons for the command, nor did He go into detail about the various ways they could be tricked into eating the fruit. That wasn't necessary, since all they needed to know was that they weren't to eat from that particular tree.

The thrust of Satan's first statement was "Indeed, has God *really* said, 'You shall not eat from any tree of the garden'?" (Genesis 3:1). Through the use of innuendo Satan was planting doubt in Eve's mind, doubt that God really had their best in mind. He was suggesting that God was holding back something good and desirable. He was also probing to find out exactly how well the woman knew God's instructions and to what degree she was committed to obeying Him. Satan uses these same strategies today. He first gets people to think that God's Word isn't true, that the Bible contains errors, that the Bible is simply a record of the religious experiences of different people, primarily the Jews.

Satan's arguments can be very subtle. For example, many people today believe that the Bible is true and without error in all matters of "faith and practice." That statement is true as far as it goes, but in many cases it masks a subtle disregard for the actual inerrancy of Scripture. The thinking Christian ought to ask certain questions. Is the Bible true when it mentions historical events? Is the Bible true when it makes observations about nature and the creation? Often the critic of the Bible will say that it has mistakes in matters of history, geography, and science, but that we can believe the Bible when it discusses spiritual matters. Unfortunately for the critic, when the Bible discusses spiritual issues they are not separated from history or creation. The spiritual issues are intimately interwoven with the historical statements, and the truth of the spiritual matter depends on the reliability of the historical or creation issue. Jesus clearly believed that Adam and Eve were real historical people and that they sinned. This was an event in history that changed history and had disastrous effects on the human race. Because of their sin Jesus, the Son of God, the second Person of the Trinity, had to come to earth to die for man's sin. If Adam had not sinned as a historical act there would have been no need for salvation.

Spiritual and Physical Truth

In John chapter 3 we have the record of Jesus' conversation with one of the most prominent religious leaders of His day, a man named Nicodemus. In the course of their conversation Jesus explained to Nicodemus that a person must be born a second time before he can see the kingdom of God. This statement stunned Nicodemus. In all his years of study he never had heard this statement, and he was confused by it. Jesus went on to explain that people are born once of their mother, but they are born sinners and spiritually dead: "What is born of flesh is flesh." Man's problem is spiritual, and he needs to be reborn spiritually.

When Nicodemus asked how this spiritual rebirth could take place, Jesus responded, "If I told you earthly things and you do not believe, how shall you believe if I tell you heavenly things?" (John 3:12). The point is that *spiritual truth cannot be separated from physical truth.* If we don't believe the Word of God when it speaks about history, geography, nature, and creation—things we can see and read about—how can we trust it when it talks about things in the spiritual realm? The Bible isn't true just when it speaks about matters of faith and practice, but it is true in *everything it says.* We must be careful not to fall into Satan's trap of believing that God's Word is only partially true.

Eve's response shows that Satan's strategy was already working. Her answer reveals that she had already begun to drift from God's command and to add to it: "The woman said to the serpent, 'From the fruit of the trees of the garden we may eat; but from the fruit of the tree which is in the middle of the garden, God has said "You shall not eat from it *or touch it*, lest you die"'" (Genesis 3:2,3, emphasis added). Eve was already accepting the idea that God was being too restrictive, and she revealed her inadequate knowledge of God's Word.

In contrast, when Jesus was tempted by Satan He used the Word accurately (Matthew 4:1-10). Satan used the same technique of misapplying the Word of God and twisting it in order to bring about confusion. But Jesus relied solely on the Word. He did not oblige Satan by entering a dialogue about theoretical possibilities. He just stuck to the Word and used it correctly. The result was that He withstood the temptation.

Has God Told Us Enough?

Another strategy of Satan is to cast doubt upon the sufficiency of God's revelation: Has God really told us enough? While there certainly is a lot more that God could have told us about a great many things, the issue is whether God has in fact told us everything we need to know. As we demonstrated in the second chapter of this book, the Bible claims to tell us everything we need to know for life and godliness (2 Peter 1:3,4). Satan's question to Eve was designed to make her doubt God's instructions and to wonder why God said what He said.

Satan's question was also designed to imply that he could give her more information about the matter, supposedly so she could make a better, more informed decision. This is still one of Satan's lures today—the idea that he has additional information which God is withholding from us, information that we need in order to deal with various situations not covered in the Bible. Such a pursuit for extra-biblical knowledge is really a criticism of God and His character. Too often the motive for "needing" more inside information is that we can check up on God to see if He has really made a wise decision for us. Once we start this line of thinking we become open to Satan's distorted perspective on a situation, which in effect is trusting Satan's word instead of God's Word. Eve should have trusted God and obeyed His simple command to not eat from the forbidden fruit, without having to know more about why God gave such a command.

The Bold Lie

Once Satan had put this suggestion in her mind and started the doubting process, he then openly stated that what God had said was not true: "The serpent said to the woman, 'You surely shall not die! For God knows that in the day you eat from it your eyes will be opened and you will be like God, knowing good and evil'" (Genesis 3:4,5). God said they would die, but Satan said they would not—that they had no reason to fear any harsh consequences for their actions.

The second part of this statement impugned the character of God. Satan stated that the real reason God did not want them to eat of the fruit was because they would become like God. In other words, God was holding back from them. God didn't really have their best interests in mind, but was simply trying to keep them from having everything they could have, trying to impede them from realizing their full potential. Now that Satan had her attention, Eve probably started wondering why God didn't want her to eat from the tree. And Satan came along with just the right answer: God doesn't want you to know everything He does because He's jealous. If you eat the fruit you will be just like Him.

This lie of Satan is still prevalent today, and is found increasingly even within the church. There are actually men who claim to be preachers of the Christian gospel who teach that people are gods—a heresy prevalent in many false religions.

The Cyanide Principle

Throughout the temptation of Eve, Satan mixed a relatively small part of a lie with a fairly substantial amount of truth. But remember that a glass of water with just one drop of cyanide in it is fatal. It isn't the water that's harmful, but the small part of cyanide. The first part of Satan's statement was a lie: God had said they would die, and Satan said they wouldn't. But the second part of his statement was true: When Adam and Eve ate of the fruit their eyes would be opened and they would become like God in the sense of knowing good and evil. In Genesis 3:22-24, after Adam and Eve had sinned and God had told them the consequences of this sin, God closed off the Garden of Eden to them. In verse 22 God said, "Behold, the man has become like one of Us, knowing good and evil." God did not say they had *become a god* but that in one particular and important way they had become *like God*, knowing (literally "determining") good and evil.

The point of the original test in the Garden was to determine whether Adam and Eve would submit to God and do what He told them and believe what He said. But Adam and Eve weren't content with that; they wanted to make up their own mind as to what was good and what was evil. By doing this they acted as if they were a god, since only God has the right to determine what is good and evil. When Adam and Eve attempted to use their own experience and reason without orienting it to God's Word, they were acting as if they were a god, and the result was catastrophic.

Satan was successful in his strategy, for he cast doubt on the truthfulness of God's Word, then on the sufficiency of God's Word, then on the personal integrity of God. Thus confused, Eve allowed herself to get in the position of trusting her own experience and reason to make the decision instead of simply obeying God's Word. This is the danger point. Once we begin to doubt either the truthfulness of God's Word or its sufficiency, we begin to rely instead on our own experience and reason. But our experience (even after all these years) and our reason (even with the completed Scriptures) are too limited and too affected by sin to ever be able to adequately handle Satan's strategies. Once we get to this point, Satan can twist us around his little finger just like he did Eve.

Entering Satan's Army

Once Eve began to look at the fruit the way Satan wanted her to, she began to desire it. She "saw that the tree was good for food, and that it was a delight to the eyes, and that the tree was desirable to make one wise" (Genesis 3:6). She then ate of the fruit. Apparently nothing happened instantly, and Eve began to think that the lie of the serpent was the truth. So she went to Adam and gave him some fruit, and he ate too. Then things changed immediately.

It was Adam's sin that was determinative. The Scriptures teach that Eve was deceived. She had been confused and duped into eating the fruit, but there was no excuse for Adam. Adam sinned knowingly: "It was not Adam who was deceived, but the woman being quite deceived, fell into transgression" (1 Timothy 2:14). Adam was the head of the race. He was the head of the family. His was the decision that made the difference. It was only after *he* ate that their eyes were opened. Would the entire race have fallen if Adam had not eaten? We can only guess at the possible outcome. The sobering fact remains that Adam *did* eat the fruit and we have been living with the consequences ever since.

When Adam chose to eat the fruit, he was choosing to disobey God and to believe and obey the serpent. At that point Adam rebelled against the authority of God and aligned himself with Satan. The result was that the human race came under the control and dominion of Satan. By declaring their independence against God, Adam and Eve enlisted into Satan's army and cast all of humanity under his command. Satan had won his victory and gained the prize. The world and the human race became legally under Satan's authority. Satan had promised them that they could be like God, without anyone telling them what to think, believe, or do.

But the horrible truth was that now they were slaves to Satan, under his rule and authority. Two key New Testament passages inform us that the unsaved person is under Satan's authority and dominion. In Acts 26:18 Jesus commissioned Paul to go to the Gentiles to preach the gospel "to open their eyes so that they may turn from darkness to light and from the dominion of Satan to God. . . ." Colossians 1:13 tells us that when a person is saved by trusting in Jesus Christ as his Savior he is delivered "from the domain of darkness." In both of these verses the literal meaning of the Greek word translated "domain" or "dominion" is *authority*. Because of Adam's choice against God, all of his descendants are born under the authority of Satan.

The Worst Kind of Death

The second thing that happened immediately after Adam and Eve ate the fruit was that they died. God had said, "In the day that you eat from it you shall surely die" (Genesis 2:17). Death in Scripture does not refer to cessation of existence, but emphasizes the idea of *separation*. Physical death is a separation from the physical world, but the soul (the essence of each person) continues to exist. Spiritual death is the separation of a person's spirit from God. This was the result with Adam and Eve, as can be seen in what immediately took place after they ate the fruit. Ultimately the unsaved soul spends eternity separated from God in hell, an eternal death.

As had been usual, God came to walk with Adam and Eve in the Garden. When Adam and Eve heard Him, rather than running joyfully to Him to spend time with Him, they hid themselves because they were afraid. They no longer enjoyed fellowship with God. Their sins had separated them from God.

Or, would it be better to say That they became "sinful?"

The second result of their disobedience was that they acquired a sin nature. They became selfish and irresponsible; their previous relationship, which had been perfectly harmonious, became torn apart. When God asked them why they hid themselves and if they had eaten of the forbidden fruit, they responded by denying what they had done and by passing the buck. Adam blamed Eve, and Eve blamed the serpent. They tried to avoid responsibility for their actions and sought to shift it to someone else. The result of their sin brought a horrible curse upon the human race, the curse of spiritual death.

The Fatal Blow

But even though God justly pronounced this curse on them, in His grace He also provided a way out, a way of salvation. God addressed the serpent and told him that He would "put enmity between you [the serpent/Satan] and the woman, and between your seed and her seed; he shall bruise you on the head, and you shall bruise him on the heel"

(Genesis 3:15). This is the first mention of God's plan of salvation. The seed of the woman refers to Jesus Christ, the Savior whom God would provide, born of a woman. Although the serpent would bruise Jesus at the cross, Jesus would deliver a fatal blow to Satan.

This is the good news that even though man rebelled against God and is born under the authority of Satan, God in His great love has provided a way of escape. The penalty for sin is death, but God provided His own Son, who would pay that penalty for man by dying on the cross in payment for their sins. "The wages of sin is death, but the free gift of God is eternal life in Christ Jesus our Lord" (Romans 6:23).

Two Vital Secrets

We must not overlook two critically important lessons. First, Satan's skill at deception was so great that people with no sin nature and who enjoyed an incredibly close relationship with God were deceived. They were tricked because they allowed Satan to direct their thinking away from God's command and to entice them into dealing with him apart from the revealed Word of God. If we are to avoid the same snare, we who *do* have a sin nature need to be even more armed with the Word of God and to make sure that we are using it accurately. Unfortunately, the superficial knowledge that most Christians have of God's Word makes them easy marks for Satan's deceptions.

Second, failure to rely solely on the sufficiency of God's Word will always lead to disaster in spiritual warfare. God is a jealous God; He wants to be trusted alone. To rely on anything alongside the Word of God is to destroy its power in our lives. That is one reason that so many Christians today lead such ineffective Christian lives and struggle so much with sin. They are merging biblical teaching with self-help techniques, psychology, drugs, unbiblical teaching about demons and sin, etc. Only by understanding what God has revealed in His Word about the enemies facing us can we erect the defenses necessary to effectively guard against them.

— 4 —

Worldview for Conquest

Do not love the world, nor the things in the world. If anyone loves the world, the love of the Father is not in him. For all that is in the world—the lust of the flesh and the lust of the eyes and the boastful pride of life—is not from the Father but is from the world. And the world is passing away, and also its lusts, but the one who does the will of God abides forever.

—1 John 2:15-17

Worldliness is one of the most difficult concepts for many Christians to understand, and because of this we continue to be vulnerable to it. Back in the 40's and 50's worldliness was often associated with certain activities. A Christian who smoked or drank alcoholic beverages or went to movies was often considered worldly. However, actions in themselves should not be classified as worldliness when viewed from the biblical perspective. When a person submits to lustful temptations and commits sinful acts such as sexual immorality, drunkenness, or gossip, these are *sins of the flesh* and not worldliness, per se.

The biblical concept of worldliness has more to do with a way of thinking, a mindset, or a worldview than with particular actions. From generation to generation the dominant worldly ideas which influence people tend to change. Satan is constantly working behind the scenes influencing the way people think—the attitudes and ideas which influence each generation. In one generation worldliness may involve an "anything goes" morality, while in another generation it may be expressed through an ultrarigid morality. Worldliness is best understood as an overall philosophy of life or way of thinking which stirs up the flesh to indulge in specific sins such as sexual immorality, drunkenness, or gossip. Worldliness often provides a rationale for sin, and it is often associated with false teachings which blind people to the truth and lead them away from God (2 Corinthians 4:4).

The New Testament contains several passages which emphasize the distinction between the Christian and the world. This contrast is so marked that James warns us that friendship with the world is hostility toward God (James 4:4). There is no middle ground or place of neutrality. In those areas where we think like the world we are hostile to God. And such worldly thinking will eventually trip us up in the sins of the flesh. Remember, we are not to be conformed to the world, but transformed by the renewing of our mind (Romans 12:2). Therefore it is critically important that we understand what the Bible means by the world, how worldliness is manifested in our present generation, what the characteristics of worldliness are, and how God tells us we can avoid worldliness.

What It Means to Be Worldly

In the New Testament, the word "world," (from which we derive our English word "worldliness" or "world-like-ness") is a translation of the Greek noun *kosmos*. It was used to signify the orderly arrangement of individual parts into an integrated whole, as of the orderly arrangement of soldiers in battle formation.

In Greek thought the concept of beauty and order were linked together. So *kosmos* often expressed the idea of a beautiful arrangement or an adornment or decoration. This was an appropriate word for the Holy Spirit to choose, since Satan loves to decorate his ideas with the most beautiful attire. We should understand "world," "worldly," and "worldliness" as the external arrangement of nonbiblical thinking (or what we called *the human viewpoint* in Chapter 2). Worldliness is an organized and attractive system of ideas, concepts, attitudes, and methods which Satan uses to compete with God's concept of how people should live on planet Earth. Satan is the head and controller of this system of thinking. Whenever we think like the world we are thinking exactly like Satan wants us to. Lewis Sperry Chafer, an outstanding Bible teacher of a previous generation, has described the world system in this way:

> The *cosmos* is a vast order or system that Satan has promoted which conforms to his ideals, aims, and methods. It is civilization now functioning apart from God—a civilization in which none of its promoters really expect God to share, who assign to God no consideration in respect to their projects. This system embraces its godless governments, conflicts, armaments, and jealousies, [as well as] its

> education, culture, religions of morality, and pride. It is that sphere in which man lives. It is what he sees, what he employs. To the uncounted multitude it is all they ever know so long as they live on this earth. It is properly styled *the satanic system*, which phrase is in many instances a justified interpretation of the so-meaningful word *cosmos*. It is literally a *cosmos diabolicus*.[1]

Worldly thinking often shapes the themes of popular television shows and movies where man is depicted exploring space to expand his empire, building his own world, searching for meaning to life, etc. but the God of the Bible is nowhere to be found.

Worldliness is often presented as something beautiful, desirable, and enlightening. As Eve thought after agreeing with Satan's temptation, "it was a delight to the eyes and . . . desirable to make one wise" (Genesis 3:6). As this verse indicates, Eve was ready, willing, and able to sin when she starting looking at things from Satan's point of view rather than God's point of view. Worldliness is Satan's window dressing, presenting evil in a way which seems like the good, right, and proper thing to do. When a person is not trusting God's Word to direct him, it is very easy for him to be deceived into adopting worldly thinking. Because Satan is a beautiful creature of God, he is able to present evil as a beautiful thing.

Three Strong Desires

Many people today speak constantly about spiritual warfare. Often their attention is focused almost exclusively on Satan and demons, even though spiritual warfare in the Bible is presented as a threefold operation against the world, the flesh, and the devil. As a result of being so preoccupied with only one phase of the battle, many Christians have suffered great infiltration on the fronts of the world and the flesh.

If we want to be successful as Christians in avoiding worldliness we must first understand its basic characteristics. First John 2:16 and James 3:15 are two crucial New Testament passages which tell us about the nature of this world-system.

In 1 John 2:16 the apostle John describes the totality of the world-system, "all that is in the world," as composed of three parts: 1) "the

1. Lewis Sperry Chafer, *Systematic Theology*, Vol. II (Dallas Seminary Press, 1948), p. 77.

lust of the flesh," 2) "the lust of the eyes," and 3) "the boastful pride of life."

The first component is "the lust of the flesh." This refers to our evil desire to satisfy the impulses which stem from our fallen nature, called "the flesh." "If it feels good, do it" is a popular slogan generated by the world a number of years ago which accurately captures the idea behind the lust of the flesh. The idea often used in commercial advertising that we deserve all the fine things in life is a worldly idea that appeals to the lust of the flesh.

Then we come to a somewhat similar phrase, "the lust of the eyes." This has to do with desire for things that we see, things which catch our eye. The emphasis is on external attractiveness without examining the underlying values. "The lust of the eyes" is associated with greed, envy, and covetousness. This type of greed is one of the major controlling principles in the world-system.

"The boastful pride of life" is cited as the third controlling principle of this world-system. It is the arrogant attitude by which people think more highly of themselves than they ought. It is the ambition to center one's life around self rather than God.

All three of these characteristics originated with Satan in his fall, were passed down to Adam and Eve, and are daily the most imitated philosophy of life on the globe today. The central idea of the world's approach to life is selfishness, summarized in three words: passion, greed, and pride. The world-system favors "men who are alienated from God [who] have [as] their ambition in life the desire to please the longings of a nature corrupted by sin; to possess the things they see and can enjoy; to prevail over their fellow-men in power and prestige."[2] These are Satan's rules for the game of life in this present world-system.

In contrast, the believer is called to live a life of love and self-sacrifice toward God and man. The world hates believers (John 15:19) because the principles of the world are diametrically opposed to that of the Christian. This is why John commands believers not to "love the world, nor the things in the world" (1 John 2:15).

James contrasts the wisdom of the world with the wisdom from above in James 3:15-17. Once again three terms are employed in this description: "earthly, natural, demonic" (James 3:15). Wisdom in the Bible means *skill in living*. It includes not only intellectual insights, but also carries the added element of knowing how to put knowledge

2. Ibid., pp. 47-48.

into practice in a skillful and successful manner. Worldly wisdom is very good at instructing unbelievers on pointers for getting ahead in this world. Perhaps a new success seminar entitled "Getting Ahead in the Cosmos" would do quite well with its three simple principles of *earthly*, *natural*, and *demonic*.

Earthly has to do with one's perspective. The wisdom of the world does not have a perspective beyond the horizon of this world. It has neither a heavenly nor an eternal perspective. It is time-bound. *Natural* refers to the nature of fallen man. For something in the Bible to be natural means that it is still in the fallen, unregenerate state, not under the influence of the Spirit of God or the spiritual. *Demonic* means just what it says: It is a wisdom in keeping with Satan's program that attempts to control us by doctrines of demons. It is a wisdom which rejects God as the source for skill in living.

Perhaps a clearer way to grasp the idea of worldliness is to see it fleshed out in the examples of the Old Testament. Since the Jews did not have a Greek word like *kosmos* of the New Testament, they developed the idea of worldliness by showing its characteristics through a nation. It is primarily through the intellectual, cultural, and spiritual heritage established in Babel that Satan molds the image of worldliness in the Old Testament. Throughout the Bible it is *Babel* and *Babylon* which epitomize worldliness.

Nimrod was a grandson of Ham, one of Noah's three sons who came to the new world on the great ark. Noah and his three sons were responsible for founding society and its new culture after the flood. Nimrod was somehow able to coerce many men of his time into forming a kingdom of his own making. Under Nimrod, sinful people quickly resumed the evil activities for which God had sent the flood.

Babel was the birthplace and center from which Nimrod's activities and the kingdom of man went forth. Babylon was the first attempt of men down through history to unify people in order to solve their common problems. In essence it was the first United Nations and the origin of the global-unity idea that is at the root of all such movements. This attempt to unite man apart from God brought down God's judgment. God confused the language of rebellious mankind and geographically scattered them across the globe in order to prevent this autonomous unification. God's confusion of language was intended to minimize the spread of worldliness by adversely impacting the communication of man's false ideas from one group of people to the next. This has served to slow down mankind's reunification in rebellion against God by causing infighting within humanity because of the differences produced by rival languages and cultures.

Even today nothing has changed. It is still man's dream to ultimately solve mankinds problems through global unity. This is clearly expressed today in the world peace movements which seek to unify mankind under a one-world government. The push toward globalism is on the rise. And yet it is this very idea that somehow man can solve his own problems apart from God which is at the root of worldliness. In the Old Testament this idea always manifested itself by human pride and defiance of God, human wisdom and knowledge, human power to control and manipulate, and vast human wealth.[3]

Pride and Defiance

First, worldliness manifests itself through *pride and defiance of God*. This is the very sin which brought Satan down, and it is the root of all sin (Isaiah 14:13,14). Babylon typified this in the ancient world. In Isaiah 47 we are given a clear picture of how the Babylonians exalted themselves as the queen of the kingdoms (verses 5,7). In their pride they thought they could provide financial and military security for their people (verses 8,9). This pride also produced its own alternate religious system, which was a mixture of astrology, divination, and sorcery (verses 9,12-15) somewhat like the contemporary New Age movement.

We see this same type of pride and defiance in our world today. Those who are promoting globalism think that human government is the solution to all man's problems and that only a one-world government will be able to provide financial security and bring world peace. More often than not these same people are promoting New Age ideas, which are a mixture of astrology, divination, sorcery, and various self-help techniques which either leave God out of the picture entirely or merely give Him lip service.

The major motivating principle used by the world and found increasingly within the church today is that of *self*. We are taught that self is the center of the universe: self-image, self-love, self-esteem, self-motivation, etc. Selfism is one of the most prominent characteristics of the baby-boom generation in America. The result has been a

3. Much of the information on Babylon is taken from Charles A. Clough, *Dawn of the Kingdom* (privately printed, 1974), pp. 14-16.

breakdown in relationships and morality. (The high divorce rate is a result of this self-oriented thinking.) This kind of orientation to self is nothing more than an expression of pride, which is the trademark of Satan and his kingdom. This type of self-orientation has bred an attitude of rejection of any external authority, especially that exerted by God. Defiance of God is increasingly becoming the norm rather than the exception.

Recently artist David Wojnarowicz displayed a picture of Christ as a drug addict in the process of injecting drugs into his arm with a syringe. The picture displayed Christ tugging with his mouth on a cord that was tightly wound around his upper arm, as used by addicts to raise their veins in order to make injection easier.[4]

Wisdom and Knowledge

The second characteristic of worldly thinking puts a high premium on *man's wisdom and knowledge* (Isaiah 47:10). This not only involves man's attempts to answer the basic questions about life through the use of autonomous philosophy but also includes astrology and other occultic arts (Isaiah 47:12,13). "All the nations were deceived by your sorcery" (Revelation 18:23).

Since modern men do not submit to God's wisdom and knowledge, man takes greater pride and satisfaction in his own thoughts. He has concluded that no one is going to save man except himself, whether by his own rational thought or by New Age mysticism. This explains why mankind has been so interested in human-viewpoint philosophy, whether of the rational variety or the mystical kind. This surely stems from pride, since historians of philosophy will be the first to admit that no one has been able to come up with a workable philosophy in all of human history, and since the lure of occult secrets has always led to bondage or been a great disappointment. However, human viewpoint says that it is the *search* for truth which is important. And so this is all that they are left with—a search having no real hope of ever finding what they are looking for.

This pride of human knowledge is often shown in the way we try to solve our personal problems. In some cases we look to humanistic psychology to find answers and help for our problems, not realizing that many of the ideas and concepts in modern psychology have their origin in demonic encounters. At other times we seek to resolve

4. Reported in *Human Events*, February 24, 1990.

difficult situations on the basis of intuitive insights. Often as pastors we have counseled people in marital difficulty who have engaged in extramarital affairs because it seemed so right to them to have this great love. They assume that God certainly wouldn't give them this great love and then expect them to walk away from it. Worldliness says "Go with your feelings," which gives the flesh a real basis for operation.

The Power to Control

A third characteristic of worldly thinking involves *the power to control and manipulate.* On the national level this is expressed through the accumulation of military and political strength. Great military and political strength is used by our modern world not merely to restrain evil but to keep people under captivity to the state and its goals. Ancient Egypt and Babylon were perfect examples of nations trusting in great military and political strength, but God humbled them both.

In answer to Pharaoh's arrogant question, "Who is the Lord that I should obey His voice to let Israel go? I do not know the Lord" (Exodus 5:2), the Lord taught Pharaoh who He was and why even rebels must obey the Lord. The Lord redeemed the Israelites out of Pharaoh's hand through the ten plagues, and in the process Egypt's great military and political strength was smashed.

In Babylon, Nebuchadnezzar asked a similar question: "What god is there who can deliver you out of my hands?" (Daniel 3:15). Nebuchadnezzar in his pride was trusting in military and political strength to coerce his subjects to bow the knee and worship him as god. Yet Nebuchadnezzar ended up realizing that "the Most High is ruler over the realm of mankind, and bestows it on whomever He wishes" (Daniel 4:25). More recently, Adolf Hitler attempted to use military and political strength to forge his Third Reich, which was to last for a thousand years. It actually lasted about ten years!

On a personal level, the pursuit of power has reached new proportions. Just think about new terminology that we commonly use: power dress, power suit, power lunch, etc. This is one of the great appeals of New Age or metaphysical thought: It promises a new *power* to its adherents. Thus seminars like FORUM (formerly est), Silva Mind Control, and ONE offer their customers new power over themselves and the ability to manipulate and control other people so that they may be more successful in their businesses. Unfortunately the power that some of their customers are introduced to is demonic.

Money As Security

Fourth, worldliness sees *the accumulation of financial wealth as the means to security and happiness in this life*. An example in the Bible seems almost contemporary. The metropolis of Tyre (Ezekiel 27) shows the classic pattern as to how vast wealth operates in Satan's world-system. The central drive behind ancient Tyre's success in the commercial world was her drive to please self—in other words, selfish ambition.

> So captivated was Tyre with her own ability that she undertook daring expeditions, bold and unprecedented voyages. With her excellent charts of the ocean, her study of the stars, and carefully guarded records as to depths and distances, winds and currents, she was able to outstrip all other competitors by sailing during the night.[5]

Pride, self-conceit, a sense of grasping, and destructive covetousness all characterized Tyre and Satan's world-system. Tyre was famous for having the greatest merchants of the world: They could get along with anyone as long as there was a dollar to be made!

Someone has said that Americans are the salesmen of the world, which explains why the pragmatist, the person who gets the job done or closes the sale, is the most admired person in our culture. We live in a time in which more and more people are in pursuit of things that only money will buy. There is an unquenchable drive toward status, fame, luxury, ease, comfort, and entertainment.

Even within the church a whole new theology of health and wealth is being proclaimed and practiced. This is a characteristic of Babylon and should be seen as the product of the spirit of this world. Wealth is not evil in itself, but the drive to accumulate wealth by any means and for the purpose of selfish desires is clearly contrary to Scripture. It is *the love of money* which is a root of all sorts of evil (1 Timothy 6:10). As with many modern Americans, wealth is pursued for its own sake. A contemporary bumper sticker reads, "Whoever dies with the most toys wins."

By now you have some insight as to how you can spot worldliness. At its very core it is the assertion of man's independence against God. It is the idea that security and fulfillment can be attained in life apart

5. Paul B. Clingen, "A Portrait of Satan in Ezekiel Twenty-Eight" (Th.M. thesis from Dallas Seminary, 1954), p. 39.

from submission to God. Nimrod and his contemporary imitators seek to solve man's problems through global unity even at the expense of personal liberty. In their assertion of their independence they turn to alternative religions, which are nothing more than thinly disguised forms of Satanism. But lest we miss the brilliance of Satan's clever designs, we should note that the goals and ideals of worldliness are always very attractive. After all, who could be against world peace, the solving of world hunger, nuclear disarmament, personal prosperity, and saving the whales? These goals are not wrong in themselves; what is wrong is the fact that modern man has chosen to solve these problems on his own while denying his need for God. At the very core of man's efforts is his rebellion against God, his desire to make a success out of planet Earth apart from God. The idea that man can solve his problems on his own appeals to "the lust of the flesh, the lust of the eyes, and the boastful pride of life."

How can we escape the influence of worldliness? First we must understand how the system really works.

How the System Works

Any of us who have been through military boot camp will never forget the experience. First the drill instructor gives us a talk about how he is in charge and how we are under his absolute authority. Then he spends the rest of the day (from a very early start!) showing us that he has authority over us by constantly yelling at us, calling us all kinds of unrepeatable names, and making us do push-ups every time we don't do exactly what he commands us to do. He exerts this kind of control over us for the entire duration of boot camp, until finally, an hour before graduation, he manages a smile and makes a speech of appreciation for our accomplishments. One thing we all know about our drill sergeant: He is in total control. The same is true about Satan's rule over his domain during this present age: *He is in control.*

The apostle Paul labels the age in which the world currently operates as "this present evil age" (Galatians 1:4).[6] It is evil because Satan is in charge of setting the agenda. Satan is said to be "the god of this world [age]" (2 Corinthians 4:4), as well as "the ruler of this

6. Much help in this section was gleaned from Allan S. Maitha, "The World: Enemy of the Believer" (Th.M. thesis from Dallas Seminary, 1970).

world" (John 12:31; 14:30; 16:11). Jesus Christ did not question Satan's right to give Him the "kingdoms of the world" if He would worship him (Luke 4:5-7). In fact, during the future tribulation period, Satan will confer authority over this world to the man of sin (Revelation 13:1-8), thus fulfilling the offer which he made to the Son of God.

During the present age, Satan has been given a certain freedom of operation, within divinely appointed limits, to act as God's opponent until the time when God will restrict him to the bottomless pit (Revelation 20:2,3), thereby removing his influence from the world. Indeed, it will be a new world when that day comes. In the meantime we should not forget that even though Satan currently occupies a high position and a certain degree of freedom, his days are numbered. God is sovereign, and His plan includes His rule over evil as well as good.

Satan rules over all the subjects under his domain, which includes both fallen angels and sinful mankind. John tells us that the scope of Satan's domain is the world: "The whole world lies in the power of the evil one" (1 John 5:19).

The fallen angels are Satan's footsoldiers, who do his bidding in the spiritual realm. They are an organized group described in Scripture as "rulers, powers, world forces of this darkness, and spiritual forces of wickedness in the heavenly places" (Ephesians 6:12).

Those who do not know Christ as Savior are said to have been caught in "the snare of the devil, having been held captive by him to do his will" (2 Timothy 2:26). Every human being is at the beck and call of Satan, unless he or she has escaped his clutches by becoming a believer. Scripture describes unbelievers as those who walk "according to the course of this world, according to the prince of the power of the air, of the spirit that is now working in the sons of disobedience" (Ephesians 2:2). All unbelievers are in bondage to Satan, making them his unwitting allies against God. He makes them dance in harmony to the tune of the world-system.

This system operates similar to the way a radio station functions. Satan is the program director who selects the agenda for the station. The demons and fallen humanity produce the programming, which propagates and reinforces the agenda (false doctrine). The station then transmits the message over the air. However, you cannot pick up the station unless you have a receiver tuned to the right frequency. Fallen humanity is all tuned in to radio station "WORLD" with the volume turned all the way up. The receiver is the flesh, which is attracted to Satan's frequency. All three work in harmony: the world, the flesh, and the devil.

The unbeliever's nature is sympathetic to the evil nature of the world-system, so the two are attracted. The main difference between the two is that the world-system characterizes the *corporate* expression of Satan while the flesh embodies these same characteristics on a *personal* level. When an individual becomes a believer in Jesus Christ this alignment is broken and all-out war begins between the Christian and the world.

Winning the Battle

Jesus told the Pharisees in the temple that "you are of this world, I am not of this world" (John 8:23). Later He said that His followers "are not of this world, even as I am not of the world" (John 17:14; see also 17:16). Christ then prayed to the Father on behalf of all believers that He not "take them out of the world, but . . . keep them from the evil one" (John 17:15). We see from the New Testament that Christ is our model for how a believer should relate to the world. The well-known slogan often heard in Christian circles is true: Believers are to be *in* the world but not *of* the world.

The reason the believer is not of the world is because he has been chosen out of the world (John 15:19) and born of God (1 John 5:18). He is a holy rebel against Satan. The believer has a new position in Christ because God has "delivered us from the domain of darkness and transferred us to the kingdom of His beloved Son" (Colossians 1:13). His new nature no longer matches up with the tune being transmitted by the world-system. The believer is now able to tune the dial to a new frequency and match up his regenerated nature with the things of the Lord. He is now "the light of the world" (Matthew 5:14). He goes from being a resident of this world to one who is a cosmic tourist (Philippians 3:20). But how is he to conduct himself and relate to the world now that he is an outsider?

The believer's new relationship to the world-system revolves around two simple aspects: *separation from the world* and *evangelism of the world.* We are left in the world to evangelize it, because in the world is the only place where we can call sinners to faith in Christ. On the other hand, we are to be separate from the world because we are citizens of a heavenly country and have a different lifestyle that we are to exhibit before the world.

Living in a Monastery?

Many New Testament passages command separation from the world. Some of them include the following: "Do not be conformed to this world" (Romans 12:2); "instructing us to deny ungodliness and worldly desires" (Titus 2:12); "keep oneself unstained by the world" (James 1:27); "friendship with the world is hostility toward God" (James 4:4); "escaped the corruption that is in the world" (2 Peter 1:4); "escaped the defilements of the world" (2 Peter 2:20); "do not love the world" (1 John 2:15).

Most Christians would agree that the Bible teaches us to separate from the world, but we would not all agree on what this means and how it should be done. One popular answer has been *monasticism*. Monastics isolate themselves from any physical contact with the outside world. Usually they build a large, stone edifice (if they are located in a populated area) and shut themselves in so that they will not come into contact with the world. They specialize in refraining from practices that they consider to be worldly. Their theory is that if they do not personally encounter the threat from the world, they will not have to deal with it. The modern commune is one such monastic approach to dealing with worldliness.

One of the problems with this approach is that the spirit of the world is usually transferred from a secular expression to a religious rite. Too often the occupants within the monastery are surprised to find that the world actually resides within each of them. Monasticism is in fact just a worldly approach to spirituality.

The New Testament teaches that we accomplish true separation from the world by conforming to our new relationship to God and to the world. This means that we will have interaction with unbelievers, but that we will live before them in such a way that they will see a difference in our attitudes and actions. Christ said in the Sermon on the Mount, "Let your light shine before men in such a way that they may see your good works and glorify your Father who is in heaven" (Matthew 5:16).

How do we do this? Since the world is out to benefit "number one" (i.e., self), we should display the opposite attitudes and actions by seeking what is best for others (i.e., love). Since the world takes God's truth and distorts it, believers should speak the truth in love. When we live a life that contrasts sharply with the lifestyle of the world, this provides a sound basis for the other aspect of our relationship to the world: effective evangelism. First Peter 3:15 incorporates these two aspects into one passage: "Sanctify Christ as Lord in your hearts [separation from the world], always being ready to make a defense to everyone who asks you to give an account for the hope that is in you [evangelism], yet with gentleness and reverence [the Christian attitude as contrasted with the worldly attitude of pride and arrogance]."

The believer separates himself from the world in two major areas: in *word* and *deeds*. The epistles of the New Testament emphasize how a believer is to think and believe and then how to live in accordance with that doctrine. This is what is meant by not being conformed to the world but being transformed by the renewing of our mind (Romans 12:2). The New Testament is full of teachings which describe the essentials of the Christian life, and usually they are followed by admonitions to live a godly life for the Lord. If a believer loses his interest in doctrine and godly living, he is in very great trouble, since there is no other effective basis to combat the world.

Shining in the Darkness

Evangelism is the other major way the believer relates to the world. Christ commanded His followers to "go into all the world and preach the gospel to all creation" (Mark 16:15). This is hard to do from within the four walls of a monastery; in order to reach people we need to be in the world where people actually are!

In evangelism, one temptation is to make the gospel appealing to the world. The gospel is then watered down and reshaped to make it attractive to worldly people. All too often Christians are drawn in by the trends and fads of the world as their platform for evangelism. If the world has success through a certain kind of music, then we incorporate the world's music as something to attract them for evangelism. If the world has social and moral problems, then we become "Christian" sociologists and psychologists in order to show them how helpful Christianity is so that they will listen to the gospel. If the world uses certain tactics to effect political and social change, then the Christians will have their own similar version—except five to ten years behind the world's!

God has already given us a platform from which to attract the world so that we can preach the gospel to them. The New Testament calls this the "light shining out of a dark place"; it is the godly behavior of the believer and the message of the gospel of Jesus Christ.

> Christ bore witness to the sinfulness of the world's conduct by demonstrating the moral perfection of God in his life; so also, by allowing the holy character of God to radiate in his life, the believer exposes the sinfulness of the world's practices, showing that they are contrary to God's holy character. Christ also bore witness to the truth by showing men who God is and what he requires of them; so also, the believer bears witness to the truth, relating the life, death, and resurrection of the Lord Jesus. In these two ways the believer fulfills his responsibility of being a witness to the world.[7]

Truly Unique

We are to relate to the world by being *different* in our lifestyles and our beliefs, not by being *similar*. They believe in themselves, we believe in Jesus Christ; their goals are earthly, our goals are heavenly; their trust is in their physical strength and beauty, our trust is in God and the Holy Spirit; they seek selfish fame and fortune, we seek selfless proclamation of Christ.

Unfortunately, many brands of Christianity today are simply worldly counterfeits. The world is materialistic, so Christians have their health-and-wealth gospel. The world holds to a situation ethic, so Christians have their licentious preachers who claim that we can go freely sin because we are forgiven anyway. The world is entranced by spirits and psychic power, so Christians give undue attention to demons, spirits, deliverance, and exorcism. The world puts its faith in psychology to solve life's problems, so Christians blend the world's answers with the Bible's and thus destroy both.

Because of our new position in Christ, John tells us that we have victory over the world: "Whatever is born of God overcomes the world; and this is the victory that has overcome the world—our faith" (1 John 5:4). We achieved victory over the false doctrine about who Christ is when we believed the gospel, but the battle is still raging. The world is in a pitched battle with us because we have become holy rebels against Satan and his world-system. Therefore the world will do everything it can to remove us from the battle, either by luring us

---

7. Ibid., pp. 99-100.

back into the fold through the attractions of the world (which still appeal to our sin nature) or by tempting us to renounce our allegiance to Christ through persecution or martyrdom. But whether tempted by bribery or torture, we have victory in Christ because He has overcome the world (John 16:33).

— 5 —

The Enemy Within

The deeds of the flesh are evident, which are: immorality, impurity, sensuality, idolatry, sorcery, enmities, strife, jealousy, outbursts of anger, disputes, dissensions, factions, envying, drunkenness, carousing, and things like these.

—Galatians 5:19-21

Russian by birth, Jewish by race, and British by choice, Sidney Reilly was perhaps the greatest spy of all time. Ian Fleming, the creator of James Bond, at one time served with the British Secret Intelligence Service. When he first created the Bond character he reportedly said that Bond was just a piece of nonsense he dreamed up—certainly no Sidney Reilly! Perhaps the most harrowing of Reilly's feats was his infiltration of the German High Command in the First World War. But his greatest task of all was his final assignment. With the threat of the Bolshevik rebellion in Russia and Russia's consequent withdrawal from the war, British intelligence sent Reilly to Russia to overthrow the Bolshevik government, a task which Reilly nearly accomplished. It took the Soviets another seven years to finally stop him. His abilities to organize and mobilize people against the Bolsheviks was unsurpassed. It is said that no enemy was more feared by Lenin than Sidney Reilly.

Reilly was feared because his allegiance was to another government. His secret activities were all aimed at subverting and overthrowing the rule of the Bolsheviks. Governments fear nothing as much as the traitor, the rebel within the camp, who covertly seeks to destroy their work. Just as governments have their traitors and spies within the camp, so Christians have theirs—the flesh.

The Internal Rebel

It is the flesh, the rebel within, that seeks to hinder and suppress the work that God is doing in our lives. In the previous chapters we have described the origin and nature of the first two enemies the Christian faces: Satan and the world. Yet these two are *external* enemies; neither one has the power to make any person disobey God. What gives these two enemies an opportunity to operate in the believer's life is the enemy that is in each of us. Satan (and demons) can tempt the Christian and the world-system can provide philosophies and ideas which give a rationale for sin, but it is the individual who makes the choices, yields to the temptation, or utilizes the philosophy in order to justify his sinful action.

From the moment Adam sinned in the Garden he acquired something new. Some may call it a principle, or a nature, or an influence, but whatever term is used, it is a predisposition, a desire, a hankering to assert one's own authority over God's. This nature has been passed on from Adam to every one of his descendants except Jesus Christ, who "knew no sin."

The first mention of the power and control of sin is found in Genesis 4 in the familiar story of Cain and Abel. When the two had brought their sacrifices to God, we are told that God had favor on Abel's, but He did not have favor on Cain's. Hebrews 11:4 tells us that the reason was because Abel's motivation was faith while Cain's apparently was not. The result was that Cain was angry (a mental-attitude sin) and his countenance fell (he was depressed). Modern man faces the problem of anger and depression and looks for the solution in many places. Yet he fails to understand that the problem is his sin nature. God analyzed the problem for Cain and gave him the solution:

> If you do well, will not your countenance be lifted up? And if you do not do well, sin is crouching at the door; and its desire is for you, but you must master it (Genesis 4:7).

The Hebrew word for "crouching at the door" carries the image of a ravenous beast ready to pounce and devour its victim. This is what the enemy within seeks. The solution, simply put here, is to master this enemy. The result is that depression and anger are conquered. The problem was not demons, nor was it a parental disappointment in early childhood; the problem was *personal sin* and the solution was *mastery of the sin nature*.

The Flesh Within

In the New Testament the word used most often to describe this sin nature is "the flesh." The clear testimony of the New Testament is

Every form of temptation must appeal to the flesh to be effective.

that the flesh, the rebel within, is the major and most influential enemy facing the Christian (cf. Romans 7:14,18; 8:1-17; Galatians 3:3; 5:13-21; Ephesians 2:3). The 21 letters in the New Testament were written to address the important issues confronting Christians in this age, the church age. It is reasonable to expect that if anything is an important issue for the believer in this age it will be given a comprehensive treatment in these letters, and that if something isn't an issue it will probably be ignored.

The silence of these letters in some areas speaks volumes. For example, demons (or evil spirits) are mentioned only ten times, and most of these simply relate to certain factual truths about demons (more about this later). On the other hand, in these same letters are over 50 references to the flesh as the primary enemy of the Christian (and "the flesh" is only *one* way that this sin nature is referred to). It is obvious that the New Testament perspective is that the major area of conflict is in the arena of the flesh.

"Flesh" in the Scriptures has three basic meanings. The first is a reference to either a body or the basic material of a body (i.e., flesh and bone). The second sense focuses more on the limitations of man in contrast to the power and ability of God. The third sense is the one we are focusing on in this chapter: the sinful nature of man. Although "flesh" sometimes refers to the physical body, and in some passages to sensual sin, it is not restricted to that meaning, but covers the entire realm of sin (Galatians 5:19-21).

When you and I were born we were in bondage to sin, "the flesh" (Romans 6:6,17). We were enslaved by it so that everything we did was marked by the flesh. Though some things we did were relatively good, the Bible teaches that we could do nothing that was good in God's eyes. Isaiah 64:6 informs us that "all our righteous deeds are like a filthy garment." Paul echoes this thought in Romans 7:18, where he says, "I know that nothing good dwells in me, that is, in my flesh." The "good" he refers to is that which is good in God's eyes. What we learn from this is that in the light of God's righteous standard everything produced by man is evil and sinful.

What Is Sin?

We must make sure we understand how the Bible defines sin. Too often people think of sin and the works of the flesh as only the baser activities, but the biblical concept of sin is much broader than that. Romans 14:23 says that "whatever is not from faith is sin." This means that any thought, word, or deed, no matter how noble, no matter how helpful, no matter how religious, if it is not done in dependence upon God (the meaning of faith), is done in dependence upon our own powers, and God calls that sin. That is exactly what Adam did in the Garden: Rather than depend upon God and what He said, he depended on his own ability to handle the situation himself. That is the essence of idolatry and self-worship.

Not only does the flesh produce the baser activities that we associate with sin, but it also produces relative good. In Philippians 3:3,4 Paul warns us from his own experience not to put any confidence in the flesh, for the flesh produces a false religion, a religion based on human ability. Paul certainly understood this phenomenon, because for years he was caught up in pursuing the religious standards of the Pharisees and hoping that these good works would have value in God's eyes. No one was more religious than Paul, but in Philippians 3:7 he states that all his good works were no better than rubbish (literally manure) compared to the true religion, which is based not on human works but on the work of Christ alone.

Besides producing evil works as well as works often thought of as good, the flesh is clearly in control of every unbeliever. This is emphasized in Romans 8:1-13.

In Romans 8 we see a contrast between the person who is living "in" or "according to" the flesh and the person who is living "in" or "according to" the Spirit. It is clear from Romans 8:9 that the person in the Spirit is a Christian: "You are not in the flesh but in the Spirit, if indeed the Spirit of God dwells in you. But if anyone does not have the Spirit of Christ, he does not belong to Him." At the moment a person trusts Jesus Christ as his Savior, God does a number of things for him. One of these is to give him the Holy Spirit, who indwells every believer. If a person does not have the Holy Spirit, then he is not a Christian. Therefore he is not "in the Spirit" but is still living according to the flesh.

The person in the flesh is in rebellion against God. He is not in a position of neutrality but, harsh as it might sound, a position of hostility. Romans 8:7 tells us that "the mind set on the flesh [the unsaved mind] is hostile toward God." The result of this hostility is that the unsaved mind rebels against anything that God commands. When we are still unsaved sinners we hate God and everything He stands for, and we are absolutely incapable of doing anything to please Him. "There is none righteous, *not even one*; there is none who understands, there is none who seeks for God; all have turned aside, together they have become useless; there is none who does good, there is *not even one*" (Romans 3:10-12, emphasis added). This point is often overlooked. It is easy for us to think that some very nice people who seem to talk a lot about God and engage in "spiritual" activities do indeed have a desire to know God or perhaps even love God. But this is not what God says. Because they refuse to know Him on the terms He has set forth in Scripture, the Holy Spirit accurately tells us that they are God-haters, and that the God they seek is a God of their own devising rather than the God of the Bible.

There Is Hope

We have taken some time to detail what the Bible teaches about the flesh because too often we take our own sinfulness somewhat lightly. In our day many people think that self is basically good—perhaps a little misguided at times, but still basically good. These passages reveal the true degradation of the human race and how we are all defiled by sin. Yet as horrible as this picture is, God's message of hope remains. When a person is saved, he is freed from this unholy dominion and the wicked hold that the flesh has over each one of us. Romans 6:18 tells us that when we are saved we are freed from sin and bondage to sin, and instead become slaves to righteousness. This doesn't mean that the flesh or our sin nature is eradicated, but simply that its tyranny is broken. The flesh controls a believer only when he allows it to. That is the whole point of Romans 6. Because the Christian has been identified with the crucifixion of Christ, "the old man," (the person he was in Adam before he was saved) is crucified, dead, and gone. The Christian is now no longer the person he once was. Instead, he is a new creature in Christ (2 Corinthians 5:17).

However, he still retains his fleshly nature. This is not removed until we die and receive our resurrected body. Romans 6:6 says, "Our old self was crucified with Him, that our body of sin might be done away with." The "old man" here is not the sin nature, but our old, unregenerate self. Ephesians 4:22,24 shows the contrast: "In reference to your former manner of life, you lay aside the old self, which is being corrupted in accordance with the lusts of deceit . . . and put on the new self, which in the likeness of God has been created in righteousness and holiness of the truth." While the English translation makes it appear that the believer is *to put off* the old man, the Greek uses a construction here that is best translated "*you have put off* the old man with his works." This is seen clearly by the parallel passage in Colossians 3:9,10: "Do not lie to one another, since you laid aside the old self with its evil practices, and have put on the new self, who is being renewed to a true knowledge according to the image of the One who created him." We must recognize that the person we were before we were saved is dead and gone, crucified with Christ. But though the *old man* is dead, the *sin nature* continues. We still have a problem with the flesh. This is why there are so many commands in the New Testament to put to death the deeds of the flesh. We should live like the new creatures that we truly are in Christ.

Salvation in Three Phases

God's package called *salvation* is implemented in three phases. Phase one occurs when a person trusts Christ as his Savior: He is freed from the penalty of sin and receives eternal life. This is known as *justification*. Phase two begins at the moment of salvation: We receive the Holy Spirit, who enables us to have victory over the sin in our life. This takes place throughout the rest of our life and is a process known as *sanctification*. It is during this phase that we learn to walk by the Spirit and have victory over the present power of sin in our life. Finally, when we go to be with the Lord and receive new bodies we will be saved from the very presence of sin. This third phase is called *glorification*.

Even though Christians are liberated from their *enslavement* to sin, this does not mean that they never sin, or that resisting sin is easy. The sin nature is still very much present and still set on asserting itself. Man's propensity to evil and rebellion against God is just as much there after salvation as before. It's just that after salvation *he has a choice*, whereas before salvation he had no choice. He was a slave to sin (Romans 6:17), he was being "corrupted in accordance with the lusts of deceit" (Ephesians 4:22), he was spiritually dead (Ephesians 2:1), and he was unable to perceive spiritual truth (1 Corinthians 2:14). Before salvation there was no choice, but after salvation we do have a choice. This is the power of the cross. The sin nature has power only if the believer chooses not to trust in God's Word and obey Him, and instead places himself in a position of obedience to his past master.

This is where the central battle in the believer's holy rebellion is taking place. The flesh is set against the Spirit and the Spirit against the flesh (Galatians 5:17). Peter tells us that these fleshly lusts wage war against the soul (1 Peter 2:11). It is not a battle that calls for demonic deliverance, exorcism, or any other sort of exotic practice which holds forth the empty promise that there will be no more struggle with a particular temptation or habitual sin. This battle takes place in your own heart. Are you going to "consider yourself dead to sin" (Romans 6:11)? This means that you must believe that sin no longer has power over you, and then live in light of that fact. It means that you must master sin (Genesis 4:7) and through the power of God you can do so. To accept any notion of the Christian life which teaches that you can have a one-time experience and never have to struggle with sin and the flesh again is to accept unbiblical fantasy.

Several years ago there was a news report about a number of immigrants from the Soviet Union who could not adjust to the freedom of the United States and so returned to Russia after a few years. A Soviet citizen is like an unbeliever: He is born into a position of enslavement to a totalitarian regime with no freedom. If he emigrates to the West he is suddenly faced with freedoms he never dreamed existed. At this point he is faced with a choice: He can either continue to live as though he had no freedom or else he can believe he is truly free and begin applying those freedoms to every area of his life. Most of us find it incredible that someone who has tasted freedom could then put himself back into a bondage relationship, yet this is exactly what many Christians are doing. Rather than living in light of their freedom from enslavement to sin, and then enjoying their freedom in Christ, in one or many areas they choose to continue living as though sin were their master.

How Do You Know If You're Holy?

Since the flesh can produce works that are dressed up in the guise of morality and spirituality, it may be difficult for a person to tell whether his good deeds are simply the result of a sin nature that excels in producing good works (counterfeit good). As usual, the Bible does not leave us in the dark regarding the answer to this important question. One passage of Scripture is particularly helpful. As you read it, you might want to use it as a checklist for your own life.

In Galatians 5:17-21 the apostle Paul describes the warfare between the Spirit and the flesh. To show which is in control, Paul lists 15 characteristics of the works of the flesh. No matter how good, moral, religious, or spiritual an activity may appear, if it is produced by the flesh, then these are some of the results it will always produce. These 15 deeds of the flesh can be divided into four groups.

The first group focuses on *sensual sin*. Immorality is based on the Greek word *porneia*, from which we get the English word "pornography." It refers to any and all sexual activity outside the bounds of marriage. This includes homosexuality, pre-marital sex, and marital unfaithfulness. Any sexual activity between two people who are not of opposite sex and married to each other falls into this category. Impurity can refer to sexual sin, but it generally includes more than immorality. Sensuality, too, is broader than immorality and would include any sexual activity not necessarily involving fornication.

This would include the many off-color jokes and sexual innuendos in so-called "family" comedies on television. Even many movies rated PG or PG-13 are filled with sexual innuendo and references to illicit sex. These movies project an image of this lifestyle that is attractive. Many of the commercials and advertisements are also meant to give sexual enticement so that you will identify with the product in that way and buy it. Many men's and women's fashions today are also designed to be sensual. All of this comes under the category of sensuality and is clearly a product of the flesh.

Idolatry—With or Without Images

The second category focuses on two activities which were typical of non-Christian religions—idolatry and sorcery. Idolatry is the worship of anything in the place of God. In ancient times, and in primitive cultures even today, people make idols as physical representatives of their gods. In America our gods are usually more sophisticated idols of the mind, but even in ancient times idolatry started as a thought in the mind before it was formed into a physical image. Since we don't usually fashion images, we often think we aren't idolatrous. Nothing is further from the truth! We still think the same kinds of idolatrous thoughts as the ancients, but we just express them in a different way: We worship success, money, career, sex, family, children, comforts, and the "good life." Any of these can take the place of God in our lives and become a god unto themselves. In one sense we are more deceived than the ancients, since at least they were usually aware of what they worshiped. The average person today would never admit that his career or his children are his god.

The second activity in this group is sometimes translated "sorcery" but actually translates the Greek word *pharmakia* (from which we get "pharmacy"). Ernest De Witt Burton in his classic commentary on Galatians says of this word:

> ...from Homer down [it] denotes a drug, whether harmful or wholesome. *Pharmakia* signifies in general the use of drugs, whether helpfully by a physician, or harmfully, hence poisoning.... In the LXX the word is uniformly employed in a bad sense, of witchcrafts or enchantments.[1]

This word encompasses all of the drug use and abuse that has become so common today. Ultimately it speaks of the reliance upon a drug (whether alcohol, cocaine, sleeping pills, or something else) to provide the joy, peace, and freedom from anxiety which can only come through a right relationship with Jesus Christ. (Of course we are not talking about the legitimate use of medications for their healing benefits.)

How Do You Get Along with People?

The third group of works of the flesh contains eight deeds which show up in personal relationships: enmities, strife, jealousy, outbursts of anger, disputes, dissensions, factions, envying. Whenever people operate in the flesh, selfishness (even if cloaked in fine motives or actions) sooner or later manifests itself. As we look at this list of deeds, we can't help but think about the large number of marriage problems and the high divorce rate among Christians today. Neither can we ignore the increase in child and spouse abuse which has become so widely recognized in the last decade. This is a manifestation of sinful attitudes and living rather than living together to serve God and glorify Him.

The first of these words is one used rarely today: enmity. This carries the idea of hostility. Fallen men are at enmity with God and at enmity with other men. The only other place that this word is found in the New Testament is in Ephesians 2:14-16, where the topic is the hostility between Jew and Gentile. Strictly speaking, in the context of the Bible, it has the definite connotation of anti-Semitism, but in broader usage it would expand to the whole idea of racial prejudice.

Strife, the second word of this group, is the practical outworking of the attitude of hostility. It focuses on the action of disruption and conflict. Like so many of these works of the flesh, it is the result of following self-serving desires rather than the desires of God.

---

1. Ernest De Witt Burton, *A Critical and Exegetical Commentary on the Epistle to the Galatians*, in *The International Critical Commentary Series* (Edinburgh: T & T Clark, 1977), p. 306.

Outbursts of anger, the third term, embodies the idea of temper tantrums or explosive bursts of anger rather than a deep, burning, long-term anger.

More Works of the Flesh

The next four words should be taken together: disputes, dissensions, factions, jealousy. Each looks upon similar works from a slightly different perspective. Each is based on self-seeking, self-serving, self-assertive attitudes which bring disruption within personal relationships from family to church. These words are all found in the description of the Corinthian church. Because they were not serving Christ, but their own ends, the result was division. However, we must remember that not all division is evil (see 1 Corinthians 11:19). While the New Testament clearly exhorts Christians to be unified (see John 17:21 and Ephesians 4:1-6,13), it is a unity based upon the clear doctrines of Scripture—a unity based *upon* doctrine and not *at the expense of* doctrine.

The final group of products of the flesh focuses on two acts that must be taken together: drunkenness and carousing. Drunkenness is clearly described here as a work of the flesh. Too often today drunkenness and alcoholism are treated as a sickness. Yet the works of the flesh are clearly the results of our own choices. While the Scriptures do not categorically prohibit the use of wine or alcohol, they are always to be used in moderation and never to the extent of producing drunkenness. While alcohol abuse may lead to a chemical dependency in some cases, the root problem is not physical, but spiritual. Initially the act was a sinful choice of the will. While the chemical dependency, or physical problem, must be treated, the problem is only partially resolved if the sin issue is not dealt with.

The second word, carousing, is one not often used today. A more fitting word in today's vocabulary would be partying—having a celebration where liquor runs free, immoral activity is freely enjoyed, and fun and pleasure are indulged in at the expense of God's glory and holiness.

This litany of sins is as contemporary as the morning paper or the folks at last Sunday's church service. It is clear from this passage that these sins are not the result of demons, Satan, or the world, but are the specific outworkings of a mindset and lifestyle that are controlled by the flesh.

The Devil Made Me Do It?

The alarming fact is that there is a growing shift in belief among many Christians that places more and more responsibility for personal sin on demons or Satan. After reading articles and books written recently, we have seen references to demons named lust, murder, envy, gossip, etc. Nowhere in Scripture is there any support for this concept, but Scripture explicitly says that these actions are a product of the flesh. In fact, as Galatians 5 clearly shows, these are not demons, but works of the flesh. This is what we mean when we say that many Christians are not being biblical in their handling of various issues.

While those who teach such things may honestly want to help Christians overcome the sin in their life, we believe that such teaching is nevertheless harmful because it gives Christians an unscriptural rationale for denying personal responsibility for sin: "The devil made me do it." Rather than accepting the responsibility for our own sin, we prefer to shift the responsibility to someone or something else. Rather than choosing the biblical solution of confessing and putting to death the deeds of the flesh, we seek to solve the problem by "binding demons" or practicing "exorcisms." Interestingly, passing the buck has been a convenient way of avoiding personal responsibility for sin ever since Adam and Eve. When God confronted Adam, Adam blamed Eve, and then Eve blamed the serpent. But God refused to accept this evasion, and leveled a judgment on them because they were the ones who chose to yield. If you are a Christian, the issue is not who presents the temptation, but whether you are going to trust God and obey Him or yield to the temptation. Christians who misplace their orientation on this matter are led astray from fighting the real enemy that Scripture says attacks in this area of warfare—the flesh.

The Deep Cave of Sin

One reason that so many Christians fall into the trap of incorrect thinking on these issues is that too many people underestimate how incredibly evil sin actually is. When we move out in the direction of sin it is like going deep into Carlsbad Caverns (since we are born in the darkness). The more we become entrenched in our sin and the more it becomes entrenched in our lives, the deeper we go into the darkness of the cave. When we are saved we gain the light of Christ, which shines in the darkness around us, but we still need to reverse our steps and move out of the cave. In our fast-food, drive-through culture we deceptively think we can achieve success over lifelong habits of sin through some sort of quick-fix solution. We mistakenly believe that if we confess our sin, repent, or feel sorrow or regret for our sin, God will somehow lift us out of the cave by some spiritual elevator to the surface. But this just doesn't happen.

What *does* happen is that by the power of the Holy Spirit and the light of God's Word we are enabled to walk back out of the cave. It is a step-by-step process. It isn't easy, but it is possible. Yet the joy that comes and the fruit that is produced along the way is truly miraculous. Unfortunately, many Christians have either tried some counterfeit gimmick to spirituality or have never really tried biblical Christianity, and have subsequently given up in failure. They then panic and turn to some quick-fix solution, and one such solution that is currently popular is to blame deep-seated sin on the demons.

Defeating the Traitor

The flesh, like a spy or traitor, seeks its advantage through deception and secrecy. It seeks to avoid detection until its job of soul destruction is complete. It never gives up or retreats in this life, although the confident hope of the Scriptures is that its activity can be brought to light and at least partially neutralized. This is done by walking in the Spirit.

In Galatians 5 we are not only given a description of how to recognize the symptoms of the flesh, but we are given instructions on how to overcome the flesh. Christians (and only Christians) can do this because the tyranny of sin has been broken by our new position in Christ. Romans 6:6,7, 15-18 tells us that we are no longer under bondage to the flesh. Since we are no longer under bondage, we are able to live in obedience to God. We achieve this as we walk by the Spirit.

In Galatians 5:16 Paul begins his instructions about the conflict between the flesh and the Spirit by simply commanding, "Walk by the Spirit, and you will not carry out the desire of the flesh." He then continues by describing the conflict between the two warring parties and by painting a vivid picture of what a person's life will be like depending on which of the two parties is in control.

The idea of *walking* involves a moment-by-moment faith in something. In the cavern analogy that we used earlier, it is that moment-by-moment walk up and out of the cave in dependence upon the light (the Holy Spirit and the Word of God). When we choose to operate in the flesh, the light goes out and we reverse the direction of our walk. Our step-by-step, moment-by-moment living is to be conducted in total reliance on the Word of God and the Holy Spirit.

We live in moment-by-moment dependence on either the Holy Spirit or the flesh. We choose to follow the impulses of the flesh or we choose to depend on the Spirit. Too often we rely on the flesh to do what only God can do, and that is why Paul had to write this letter to the Galatian church. They had adopted the Mosaic law from the Old Testament as their standard for living, and were thereby attempting to live in reliance on the flesh. In this letter Paul warns the Galatians that this is attempting to do through our own power what only God can do through the Holy Spirit (Galatians 3:3).

Anyone, even unbelievers, can live a life that superficially appears to be in conformity to God's standard. But we know from Scripture that this is done through dependence on the flesh. The Christian must know that he is not to try to live out his life in the power of the flesh. If he does, this will eventually manifest itself through the works of the flesh.

The walk by the Spirit is further clarified by the statement in Galatians 5:18, "If you are led by the Spirit, you are not under the Law." Because of the phrase "if you are led," some may think that a Christian has an option in deciding whether to be led by the Spirit. But this is not the case, since every person who has received Christ as Savior has been permanently indwelt by the Holy Spirit. From the point of salvation the Holy Spirit continually leads the believer. Romans 8:14 tells us that "all who are being led by the Spirit of God [all Christians]... are sons of God." The context indicates that this is a leading in truth and holiness. Since we become children of God only when we receive Christ as Savior (John 1:12), we can be confident that the Spirit constantly leads us. *The issue is not whether we are being led but whether we are following.*

A New Understanding

When Jesus was preparing His disciples for the time when He would no longer be with them, He promised to send the Holy Spirit, who would guide them into all truth (John 16:13). This was fulfilled on the Day of Pentecost, as described in Acts 2. Once the Holy Spirit came, the new organism known as the church began, and with it a whole new era in God's program.

Whenever a person in this age trusts Jesus Christ as his Savior, the Holy Spirit immediately comes to live in him. At this same time the Holy Spirit also provides the ability to understand God's Word. This isn't some kind of mystical knowledge, and it isn't just picking up the Bible and immediately understanding it, although for some passages of Scripture that may be true. What this basically means is that *we who were blind to spiritual truth and unable to understand the Word of God are now given the capacity to understand it.* As we study the Word, learn it, and meditate on it, the Holy Spirit enables us to understand it, and He applies it to our lives. Often our understanding of some of the more difficult issues in Scripture may require years of study before we understand them accurately. Theologians call this "the illuminating ministry of the Holy Spirit." It is not a guarantee of infallibility when we interpret Scripture, but a new, Spirit-directed capacity to understand what we could not understand before we were saved.

This new capacity enables us to understand the truth of God's Word and put it into practice. Throughout the New Testament there is an important relationship between the Holy Spirit and the Word of God; both are said to be the means by which Christians grow. The Holy Spirit is the One who works in us and leads us, while the Word of God is the means that He uses to bring this about. They are best friends, and never travel alone. In addition, they never have an argument; they always agree. After all, the Holy Spirit is the agent used by the Father to write the Scriptures, so He knows them quite well! Therefore the Holy Spirit would never lead anyone to do anything which conflicts with the written Word of God, no matter how convincing the circumstances or intense the experience.

The Mechanic's Tools

Suppose we took a dented-up, poorly running 1957 Chevy to an auto mechanic for renovation. Our lives when we come to Christ may be compared to that Chevy; for years we have been living in the flesh, and our lives reflect that fact. When we are saved we do not automatically get a new set of ideas in our mind and a new set of circumstances. We have been regenerated, but now we need to be transformed. Regeneration is the work of God in us that gives us a new nature and makes us willing to be transformed. It is the Holy Spirit, like the auto mechanic, who transforms the wreck of our lives into something glorious for God.

If we took that old Chevy to a mechanic, no matter how talented and no matter how experienced, and expected him to renovate the car with only a screwdriver and hammer, we would be laughed out of the garage. The mechanic personally has the ability to perform the task, but he is limited by the tools we allow him to use. The same is true of the Holy Spirit. The tools He uses to transform our lives are found in the Word of God. The more tools we let Him use, the more equipped He is to perform the task. This is why we are commanded to renew our minds (Romans 12:2) and to let the Word of Christ dwell *richly* within us (Colossians 3:16). The failure by many Christians to allow the Holy Spirit to use all the necessary tools is one of the major reasons why these same people often think that Christianity and the solutions of the Bible do not work. They then turn to a new experience which is supposed to enable them to deal with their problems, or they start to think that the Bible needs help from another source, such as psychology, to really help them with their problems.

The Spirit of God leads us through the Word of God. By learning God's Word we give the Spirit the tools to renovate and transform our life. This takes place in two ways. First, when we encounter temptation, the Holy Spirit brings to our mind what the Bible teaches regarding that sin. When we choose to yield to the temptation and sin, we grieve the Spirit. Second, the Spirit leads us through conviction, which takes place through our conscience to the degree that our conscience has been transformed by the new standards of God's Word. When we refuse to yield to temptation by applying what we have learned from the Word of God, spiritual growth takes place. We are now on the road to maturity, increasingly able to "discern good and evil" (Hebrews 5:14). If we sin, when we are convicted by the Spirit we need to turn away from our sin and back to God. Part of this turning involves confessing our sin, which according to 1 John 1:9 is to be a standard characteristic of the Christian life.

The secret to controlling the flesh is *learning the Word of God*—letting it transform our lives and then living in accordance with this new standard. This is what it means to walk by the Spirit.

Nine Kinds of Fruit

Over a period of time, walking by the Spirit (just like walking by the flesh) will produce certain results, called fruit. The ninefold fruit of the Spirit is described in Galatians 5:22,23. These nine character traits are evident in the life of the Christian who is walking by the

Spirit. God has given us these checklists so we can evaluate our lives to see if we are walking by the Spirit or the flesh.

Love, the first fruit of the Spirit, is often misunderstood today. This is not an emotional or sentimental word. In the Greek language several different words are used for love, each focusing on a different shade of meaning. The word used here is *agape*, which connotes a mental attitude of selfless concern for others rather than an emotional attachment. The best description of this love is found in 1 Corinthians 13 and in Christ Himself (John 3:16; Romans 5:8).

The second fruit of the Spirit is *joy*. This is neither happiness nor exuberance, but a kind of stable, uplifted mental attitude that is neither disturbed nor upset by shifting circumstances. It is the attitude that Christians are to have when they face difficulties and suffering.

Peace is next. Most often in Scripture this word is used to indicate the opposite of anxiety. It is not a reference to world peace, military peace, or political peace, but a reference to a mental attitude that is relaxed and untroubled by worry and anxiety because it rests in the care and provision of God (Philippians 4:6,7).

Patience has the idea of long suffering or not responding to immediate threats, but giving people time to change and come around. The perfect example of this is the patience that God has with us. This patience is manifested toward both people and events. This is not some grim, bleak hanging-in-there attitude but is linked with joy and peace.

Kindness and *goodness* are closely related ideas. Kindness is the attitude and goodness is the action. Kindness is in some sense related to patience. It is an attitude of courtesy, respect, and consideration for people. Goodness describes the gracious actions toward others that are motivated by kindness.

Faithfulness expresses the idea of loyalty and consistency—values sorely needed in contemporary society. This includes loyalty to God, loyalty to one's spouse, loyalty to one's children, and loyalty to the church. Too often commitments in these areas are honored only when convenient. Faithfulness is demonstrated when the commitment to these areas is neither convenient nor pleasant.

Gentleness is sometimes translated "meekness." To be gentle or meek is too often pictured as being a wimp or a doormat, but nothing could be further from the biblical concept. The biblical idea of meekness is often contrasted with pride or arrogance, a central characteristic of the world-system. In this sense meekness is synonymous with humility. We must be reminded that "God is opposed to the proud, but gives grace to the humble" (James 4:6). Gentleness flows from recognizing who we are and submitting to God. This is in direct opposition to the self-assertive works of the flesh.

The last fruit of the Spirit mentioned is *self-control* or self-mastery. This particular type of self-discipline is often associated with the control of sexual desire, but it also applies to every other area of life. As we continue to grow and to develop godly habit patterns in our life, the Holy Spirit strengthens our ability to master our sinful self and to control those fleshly desires so that we do not give in to sinful temptations.

The sin problem we so often struggle with is the direct result of yielding to our own sinful nature. It is the flesh that wars against the soul. It is the flesh that is drawn and attracted to the temptations of the world and Satan. It is the flesh that is weak. Since neither Satan nor the world-system can cause us to sin, the secret of deliverance lies in learning to walk in moment-by-moment, step-by-step dependence on the Holy Spirit.

— 6 —

Invasion of the King

If I cast out demons by the Spirit of God, then the kingdom of God has come upon you.

—Matthew 12:28

Nolan Ryan is one-of-a-kind. Never before in the history of major league baseball has there been a power pitcher who has maintained a 95-mile-per-hour fastball at the age of 43 and counting. A few pitchers have lasted that long, but no one before Nolan Ryan has been able to maintain that kind of effective velocity on his fastball.

Jesus Christ is also one-of-a-kind, except infinitely greater. Never before or since in the history of mankind has there ever been a man who was also God. If Nolan Ryan is special in the field of baseball, then to an infinite degree Jesus Christ is unique to the human race. There has never before been anyone like Him, and there will never again be anyone like Him. Jesus Christ is truly an infinite, eternal one-of-a-kind.

Jesus Christ was sent on a one-of-a-kind mission to the earth by God the Father. He came to do a number of unique things, but chief among them was to live a perfect life so that He might die as a perfect sacrifice. No one else could have done this—certainly not any other human being. Christ willingly came to earth and fulfilled His mission: to set us free from the power of sin and Satan, thereby making us holy rebels against Satan and his worldly kingdom.

The Unique Ministry of Christ

When it comes to establishing a biblical basis for many of the current deliverance ministries, many of them attempt to model their ministries after Christ's unique ministry, in which He came into direct conflict with Satan and his demons. But there are events in the life of Christ that are unique to His special, one-of-a-kind ministry. While we are to be Christlike in emulating His *character*, many of the specific things He said and did were related to His special, one-of-a-kind ministry as the God-man who came into the world to save sinners. How then do we distinguish those aspects of the life of Christ which we are to build upon from those which were part of His unique messianic ministry and which He alone was called upon to do? We believe that the New Testament Epistles were given to provide instructions on how Christians are to live during the current church age. Therefore the Epistles instruct believers only in those things which they have been specifically called upon and equipped by God to do. It is for this reason that nowhere in the Epistles are there commands or examples relating to the exorcising of demons (more about this later).

While we are called to imitate the *character* of Christ, many of His miracles and His conflicts with the powers of darkness are related to His one-of-a-kind messiahship. They are not a pattern for the types of direct encounters with demons that many people within the deliverance movement claim. While it is true that believers today are tempted as was Jesus the Messiah, and that we are involved in spiritual warfare, we are to engage in warfare in a somewhat different way, as we will seek to demonstrate in the next chapter.

One reason that many people get into trouble in spiritual warfare is because they fail to understand why Jesus encountered demons during His walk on earth and why these events are recorded for us. We will have a proper perspective of spiritual warfare only if we understand the purpose behind the one-of-a-kind ministry of Jesus.

Messiah Comes to Israel

The Gospel of Matthew was written to answer the primary question which the Jews had about the messiahship of Jesus: "If Jesus the Nazarene is really the Messiah, then where is the messianic kingdom?" Many Jews had wrongly concluded that Jesus was not the Messiah because the messianic kingdom had not yet arrived. However, Matthew explains why the messianic kingdom did not come: It wasn't because Jesus is not Messiah, but rather because Israel rejected their King because of their unbelief, and there cannot be a kingdom without a King. This is why the book of Matthew builds toward chapter 12 and the famous confrontation between Christ and the Pharisees, who accuse Christ of performing His miracles by the power of Beelzebul (Prince of the demons) or Satan (12:22-37).

At this point Christ notes that Israel was committing the sin of "blasphemy against the Spirit" (Matthew 12:31) by rejecting the Holy

Spirit's testimony that Jesus was Israel's Messiah. His claim to be the Messiah had been certified through His many signs, wonders, and miracles, which included His power over Satan and demons, as the immediate context reveals (12:22-37). Not even the Pharisees could deny this fact. Therefore, instead of questioning the authenticity of the miracles of Jesus, they credited the source of His miracles to Satan rather than God. Anything but admit the truth—that Jesus was the promised Messiah.

Matthew contrasts this unbelief with the belief of John the Baptist in chapter 11. What gave rise to the expression of John's faith were the incidents related in Matthew 10. There we are told that Jesus gathered His disciples and gave them "authority over unclean spirits, to cast them out..." (10:1) so that they could go throughout Israel announcing that the King was there ("the kingdom of heaven is at hand"—10:7). What was the confirming evidence which would demonstrate to the lost sheep of the house of Israel that Jesus was the Messiah? The ability to heal and cast out demons.

After this event John the Baptist, who had been incarcerated by Herod, sent word to Jesus, asking if He was indeed the Messiah. Jesus responded by pointing to the confirmatory signs: "The blind receive sight and the lame walk, the lepers are cleansed and the deaf hear, and the dead are raised up, and the poor have the gospel preached to them" (Matthew 11:5). The parallel passage, Luke 7:21, also includes the casting out of demons. John's response clearly shows why these signs and wonders, including demonic deliverances, were performed: He believed. But his belief was in stark contrast to the unbelief of the Pharisees. When they saw the miracles of Jesus they could not dispute them, so they attributed them to Satan. The point we dare not overlook is that *Jesus' encounters with the demons were directly related to His claim to be the Messiah and His offer of the kingdom.*

Preview of the Kingdom

Most readers have undoubtedly seen a movie preview, either on television or while attending another movie. The movie preview is designed to show something of what the movie is like, but not too much, so that you will have enough curiosity to want to see that particular movie. The preview is designed to make a strong appeal so that you will decide that you want to see the movie itself. In a certain sense this is one of the purposes for Christ's first coming, and it helps explain some aspects of His ministry.

One of the major reasons Christ demonstrated He had power over sickness, nature, and the spiritual realm (including Satan and demons) was to show what the messianic kingdom would be like if Israel would accept Jesus as their Messiah. But the kingdom would not come until the nation of Israel acknowledged that Jesus was their King. Instead, they rejected Him by choosing the rebel Barabbas in place of Jesus, and said concerning Christ, "We do not want this man to reign over us" (Luke 19:14). Jesus said just before He gave the Olivet Discourse (Matthew chapters 24 and 25), "Your house [Israel's temple] is being left to you desolate! For I say to you, from now on you shall not see Me until you say, 'Blessed is He who comes in the name of the Lord!'" (Matthew 23:38,39).

Israel's kingdom was related to their response to the messiahship of Jesus. Because they rejected Him, the messianic kingdom was postponed until the yet-future time toward the end of the great tribulation when they will say, "Blessed is He who comes in the name of the Lord!"

The apostle Peter made a similar point to his fellow Jewish countrymen in Acts 3:19-21: "Repent therefore and return, that your sins may be wiped away, in order that times of refreshing [the messianic kingdom] may come from the presence of the Lord; and that He may send Jesus, the Christ [Messiah] appointed for you [Israel], whom heaven must receive until the period of restoration of all things about which God spoke by the mouth of His holy prophets from ancient time." Christ's first coming upon the earth did not result in the coming of His messianic kingdom. Even though Christ offered it, and showed previews of what that time would be like, Israel rejected the King and thus the kingdom was postponed.

By taking power and authority over Satan, demons, sickness, and disease, Christ gave a preview of the glorious conditions that will exist during the messianic kingdom, when the effects of the curse (satanic oppression and sickness) will be lifted for a thousand years. How does this impact our study of Satan and demons? We shall see as we examine Christ's interaction with demonic forces during His first coming.

Stirring Up the Insects

In parts of Texas during the summer you can look out at a field of Johnson grass and everything appears to be calm and inactive. However, when you walk through that field you stir things up. Often a wave of grasshoppers and other insects spring into action as you plod through the field. Some may cling to your clothing as you pass through, and on occasion you may come upon a jackrabbit or two or even a rattlesnake. What causes this kind of activity? Just the presence of a human being walking nearby. It upsets the normal, hidden activities which had been going on in this field of grass.

The same was true of Christ's ministry. Often it was just His presence passing through the land of Israel that caused the activity of the demonic realm to become noticeable. The activity was there all along, but our Lord's messianic presence stirred up the spiritual realm and brought that activity out into the open. On one occasion a demon asked Christ, "Have You come here to torment us before the time?" (Matthew 8:29). Yes, Christ had come to stir things up at His first coming, but He will bring final victory in the future, when the messianic kingdom arrives. Much of the demonic activity in Israel during that time can be attributed to the mere presence of Christ, the God-man.

That this heightened confrontation with the demonic realm during Jesus' life was related to His unique ministry is further seen by studying the way and frequency with which the New Testament talks about demons. The Greek word for "demon" (*daimonion*) and its related words are used 77 times in the New Testament. Sixty-seven times the word is found in the four Gospels, seven times in the Epistles, and three times in Revelation.

A similar proportion is found in the 42 times that the synonym for demons, "evil/unclean spirits," is used: 23 times in the Gospels, 13 times in Acts, three times in the Epistles, and three times in Revelation.

The Three-Part Plan

The frequency and way in which the New Testament handles issues relating to the demonic is not consistent with the thinking and practice being advocated by many people in contemporary deliverance ministries. We are not setting one portion of the New Testament against another; instead, because these two sections are harmonious, we must recognize that the Epistles do not warn believers to look out for demon-possession, nor do they describe how to become engaged in a deliverance ministry. Yet these activities were central to the ministry of Christ and to a lesser degree the apostles. Why is this the case?

We think one of the primary reasons that 87 percent of the 119 references to demons occur in the historical section (Gospels and Acts) of the New Testament is because they are tied to the unique, one-of-a-kind events associated with the messianic mission of Jesus and the beginning and establishment of the church. Complete victory over Satan and the demonic realm is scheduled to occur only when the messianic kingdom arrives. Jesus came to offer Israel this kingdom, but Israel rejected their King and His kingdom. Therefore the messianic kingdom is delayed during the current church age, until after Christ's second coming brings the removal of Satan and the demonic from His thousand-year rule upon this earth. However, because Christ was on the earth during His first coming, He was engaged in direct battle with Satan and the demonic, while during His current absence the battle is carried out indirectly, or defensively, as we shall show in later chapters.

Let there be no mistake: Christ secured complete victory at the cross over Satan and the demonic. Christ's victory, like all of history, is being implemented in progressive stages. *Phase one* of salvation is when we become a believer, at which time we receive the forgiveness of all our sins (past, present, and future) in a moment of time. During *phase two* we live the Christian life; we are still able to sin, but we are also able not to sin. It will not be until *phase three*, when we receive our new, resurrection body which is free from sin, that we will be totally and absolutely free from all aspects of sin.

God's plan is certain and sure, since the price of our full redemption has already been paid by Christ on the cross. It is not an issue of whether He can do it; rather, His plan is being accomplished in different phases. So it is with Christ's victory over Satan and the demonic: It is being carried out in phases. This fact is crucial to understanding what is going on when Christ encounters Satan and the demonic in the Gospels.

Now let's take a closer look at how Jesus dealt with the powers of darkness.

Satan Attacks Jesus

At the beginning of His ministry, Jesus Christ went into the wilderness to pray and fast for 40 days (Matthew 4:1-11). At the end of this fasting period Satan appeared and tempted Him three times. When tempted, Christ countered Satan with Scripture but did not enter into extended dialogue with him. On the third temptation Christ rebuked Satan and told him to be gone. Satan left immediately, and no extended dialogue or argument ensued.

It is important to note that Satan did not try to cast a mystical spell over Jesus in order to bind Him to his will as though He were a mere robot. Instead, the force of Satan's temptations was based on the intended compulsion of his arguments. Argument number one was an attempt to flatter Christ because He is God's Son (Matthew 4:3). In argument number two Satan tempted Christ to put on a show of His miraculous power by leaping off the pinnacle of the temple (Matthew 4:5,6) and having the angels rescue Him, thereby gaining fame and notoriety. In other words, Satan attempted to get Christ to act by Satan's methods. Christ parried this argument by accurately quoting and using Scripture: "You shall not put the Lord your God to the test" (Matthew 4:7 quoted from Deuteronomy 6:16).

In the third argument Satan offered Christ the whole world if Christ would worship him (Matthew 4:8,9). Christ's short and pointed response in verse 10 was an accurate use of Deuteronomy 6:13, "You shall worship the Lord your God, and serve Him only." At no time did Christ (unlike Eve) give in to the logic of Satan's temptations. Instead, Christ saw through the false mentality of Satan and countered with God's way of thinking. The nature of this encounter was not a mystical one, two sorcerers attacking each other with their magical powers, as is often depicted in contemporary cartoons.

Christ's handling of Satan's temptations is the exact pattern of dealing with such temptation that is prescribed in the Epistles for believers. Since the force of Satan's temptation was in the logic of what he was saying, Christ dealt with the attack by accurately countering with God's Word. Though Satan used Scripture, he used it inaccurately. Jesus countered with the *accurate* use of Scripture. Since Satan and his demons are still tempting God's people during the church age by spewing out false ways of looking at life's issues, Christ's handling of the temptation serves as a model for how believers can stand firm and counter the attacks of Satan and the demonic. This is the pattern laid out in the Epistles as well.

Binding and Loosing

Some years ago we witnessed a "deliverance" service conducted by a well-known pioneer in the field. Many bizarre things happened at the service. Many of the demons had names, such as the demon of lust, gluttony, worry, gossip, and criticism. One demon was even named after a particular food.

The "deliverance" evangelist had a routine which he would follow in casting out demons from people. First he would find out a little about the individual. He would then ask him what his problem was. (He always assumed that it was caused by a demon rather than some other source.) Then he would speak authoritatively to the demon and command the demon/s to manifest themselves. Having done this, he would usually carry on a conversation with the demon, often quite humorous, as he would insult, question, and finally command the demon to leave in the name of Jesus and by the power of the blood of Christ. Some demons would require several conversations before they would finally leave. One of the things he always did when he was commanding them to depart was to bind them and send them to the "pit of hell."

The practice of binding Satan and/or the demons and evil spirits is not only something which some Christians do during public and private deliverance sessions, but it is often a personal activity exercised on a regular basis by a growing number of Christians. Sometimes a person will pray that Satan will be bound from blinding a person to whom he or she is presenting the gospel in the belief that this will improve the likelihood of the listener trusting Christ as his Savior. Or someone might pray that an upcoming event would be protected from the influence of the demonic by binding the demons from having influence in relation to that event. On other occasions people attempt to bind Satan and his demons from certain geographical locations, such as a new house the person will be moving into, a new church building, or a particular location in a city or neighborhood. Doing this, it is believed, could affect the power and moving of God in the lives of believers as well as unbelievers.

This practice is viewed by many people as a central practice of successful spiritual warfare. Let's look at the primary Bible passages from which those who hold this belief say they have a scriptural mandate for such a practice.

Mandate for Binding?

The misinterpretation of three passages in Matthew form the primary basis for the popular "binding" teaching and practice. First we will consider Matthew 12:29, in which Jesus said, "How can anyone enter the strong man's house and carry off his property unless he first binds the strong man?" This statement by Christ was made as part of an illustration meant to refute the Pharisees' claim that Jesus "casts out demons only by Beelzebul the ruler of the demons" (12:24). The Pharisees did not want to admit, as many of the people were beginning to suggest, that Jesus was the Son of David (12:23). Therefore they attributed His exorcisms to an alliance with Beelzebul, the only other supernatural alternative in the universe. Christ replied that He is more powerful than Satan, and pointed out that one would have to control the strong man before his house could be robbed. The logic is that Christ was not in league with Satan, but was accomplishing His exorcisms by the true power of God. It would be wrong to conclude from this passage that Christ was laying down a universal pattern for believers to follow. Instead, this was a historic illustration of Christ's personal power over Satan.

There is coming a day when the strong man will be bound, along with his demonic host, and we do not have to speculate as to when that will be. Revelation 20:1-3 says that Satan will be bound for 1000 years shortly after Christ's second coming. Following the millennium, Satan will be deposited into the lake of fire for all eternity (Revelation 20:10). In the meantime, during the current age, Satan is "a roaring lion, seeking someone to devour" (1 Peter 5:8). The antidote for the believer is not to bind him, but, as 1 Peter 5:9 instructs, to "resist him, firm in your faith." *Jesus Himself* will bind the strong man, Satan, on behalf of His followers at a future time. He does not use believers to act on His behalf in this area.

The Keys of the Kingdom

The focus of the Matthew 16:19 and 18:18 passages are on the word "bind" *(deo)*. How is this word used in context and what does it mean? The word has the basic meaning of "to tie up by binding." The result is inactivity on the part of the one bound. In Matthew 16:19 and 18:18 the word bind is used with its opposite, "loose." In these contexts the idea of binding and loosing has the force of the judicial notion of "forbidding" and "permitting." This phrase was used in Christ's day by Israel's religious leaders regarding what was forbidden (bound) and what was permitted (loosed). This is why our Lord told Peter that He would give him "the keys of the kingdom of heaven; and whatever you shall bind on earth shall be bound in heaven, and whatever you shall loose on earth shall be loosed in heaven" (Matthew 16:19).

Peter was to become one of the apostles upon whom the Christian church would be founded (Ephesians 2:20). Therefore Peter and the apostles would be the human agents through whom entrance into the kingdom of heaven would be denied or allowed, depending upon whether or not one's key matched the lock. The words "shall be bound" and "shall be loosed" as used in the Greek mean that the binding and loosing in heaven will precede the binding and loosing on earth.

A translation which brings out this aspect of the original Greek would read as follows: "I will give to you the keys of the kingdom of the heavens, but whatever you bind on earth is that which shall already have been bound in the heavens, and whatever you loose on earth is that which shall already have been loosed in the heavens." Peter was to bind things upon the earth, but only what had already been bound in heaven. Peter was to set the standard on earth for entrance into the kingdom of heaven based upon the standard which God had already set in heaven. Peter was to be a mediator of the Word of God between God and man, and that standard is what Peter stated in Matthew 16:16, namely, that Jesus was "the Christ, the Son of the living God."

Affirming God's Will

"Binding and loosing" are used in exactly the same way in Matthew 18:18: "Truly I am telling you, whatever you may bind upon the earth shall be that which has already been bound in heaven; and whatever you may loose upon the earth shall be that which has already been loosed in heaven" (literal translation). Jesus is saying that believers can have confidence that when they justly excommunicate someone on earth, they are fulfilling the will of God which has already been determined in heaven. This should give them confidence in what they are doing. So in this context binding and loosing carry the idea which corresponds to our modern judicial language of declaring someone guilty (binding) or innocent (loosing). The court decision does not make someone guilty or innocent, but simply determines whether his past acts violate or conform to God's heavenly standard.

In both passages neither word is referring to the contemporary idea of binding Satan or the demonic. Instead, these references refer to carrying out God's heavenly will upon earth as it has already been determined in heaven. In fact, the contemporary idea of binding and loosing has more in common with the methods related to the casting and removal of spells found in the occult than with anything related to biblical Christianity. This is why we as believers need to be extremely careful when we adopt practices which are not mandated by the Scriptures. One scholar in commenting on these two passages has said:

> A purely magical binding and loosing such as may be found elsewhere in Greek and Rabbinic usage [passages outside of the Bible] is ruled out by the context. Jesus does not give to Peter and the other disciples any power to enchant or to free by magic. The customary meaning of the Rabbinic expressions is equally incontestable, namely, to declare forbidden or permitted, and thus to impose or remove an obligation, by a doctrinal decision.[1]

Neutral Practice?

Someone might say that this is a neutral practice that can be used either for good or for evil. This is the same logic often used in magic. Those who believe that they are using magic to do good call it white magic, while an evil use of magic is called black magic. The problem is that the Bible does not teach the use of this technique at all. It is an unproven assumption that extrabiblical practices can be used for good. The Bible teaches us to do God's will in God's way. We are not saying that everyone who uses this approach is necessarily flirting with the occult, but we are saying that it is possible for sincere use of this technique to result in the occult practice of casting and countering spells, since the Bible does not advocate this type of technique.

From Revelation 20:2,10 it appears that this kind of direct conflict with Satan and the demonic is carried on in the heavenly realm, not the earthly. God either directly moves to limit Satan and the demonic or else He uses His elect angels to accomplish His will in this regard. As we shall show in the rest of the book, God's strategy for humanity is to deal with the specific issue or sin through which Satan and the demonic may be attacking us, and to deal with that sin or issue directly. When we obey God's will relating to the issue, God and His angels will deal with Satan and the demonic behind the scene.

Christ's Conflict with the Demonic

Demonic-related material occurs on 11 occasions in the first three Gospels. It is helpful to notice the following breakdown of this material (parallel passages in parentheses). Three *general* statements about casting out demons: 1) Matthew 4:24 "... they brought to Him

1. Friedrich Buchsel, *Theological Dictionary of the New Testament*, Vol. II (Grand Rapids: Eerdmans Publishing Co., 1964), p. 60.

all who were ill, taken with various diseases and pains, demoniacs, epileptics, paralytics; and He healed them" (cf. Mark 3:10; Luke 6:17-19); 2) Matthew 8:16: "When evening had come, they brought to Him many who were demon-possessed; and He cast out the spirits with a word, and healed all who were ill (cf. Mark 1:29-34; Luke 4:38-41); 3) Luke 7:21: "At that very time He cured many people of diseases and afflictions and evil spirits; and He granted sight to many who were blind."

Seven *specific* incidents are also described: 1) Mark 1:23-28 (cf. Luke 4:33-37); 2) Matthew 8:28-34 (cf. Mark 5:1-20; Luke 8:26-40); 3) Matthew 15:21-28 (cf. Mark 7:24-30); 4) Matthew 17:14-21(cf. Mark 9:14-29; Luke 9:37-43); 5) Luke 8:2; 6) Matthew 12:22 (cf. Luke 11:14); 7) Luke 13:10-21. Two passages cover the disciples and the demonic: 1) Matthew 10:1-16 (cf. Mark 3:13-19; Luke 9:1) and 2) Mark 6:7,13. One incident of teaching was related to the Pharisees' accusation that Christ's power came from Beelzebub (Matthew 9:32-34; 12:43-45; cf. Mark 3:22-30; Luke 11:14-26).

In the first section we see three general statements relating to Jesus' casting out of demons. In the first incident many people were bringing the sick and demon-possessed to Jesus, and He was healing them and casting out "many demons" (Mark 1:34). The purpose for these events was to demonstrate that Jesus was the Son of God, as some of the demons were testifying (Luke 4:41). This is consistent with the purpose of the first three Gospels: to demonstrate that Jesus was the Messiah because He had power and authority over the demonic realm.

One of the reasons this is significant goes back to the first prophecy about the Messiah in the Bible, found in Genesis 3:15: "I will put enmity between you and the woman, and between your seed and her seed; he shall bruise you on the head, and you shall bruise him on the heel." The Messiah was supposed to be someone who would gain victory over Satan, and Christ was demonstrating to His watchers that since He had power and authority over Satan and the demonic, He was the promised Messiah.

When Jesus would cast out the demons many were "crying out and saying, 'You are the Son of God!' And rebuking them, He would not allow them to speak, because they knew Him to be the Christ [the Messiah]" (Luke 4:41). This is in stark contrast to many people within the contemporary deliverance ministries who carry on conversations with demons. Generally Christ did not permit them to speak, or even to convey the truth that He was God's Son, apparently because He did

Summary of Jesus' Ministry to the Demonized

Category		Scripture	
	Matthew	Mark	Luke
Three *general* statements of casting out demons	8:16	1:29-34	4:38-41
	4:24	3:11	6:18
			7:21
Five *specific* incidents described		1:23-28	4:33-37
	8:28-34	5:1-20	8:26-40
	15:21-28	7:24-30	
	17:14-21	9:14-29	9:37-43
			8:2
	12:22		11:14
			13:10-21
One incident of teaching related to the Pharisees' accusation that Jesus' power came from Beelzebub (Satan)	9:32-34 12:43-45	3:22-30	11:14-26
Two occasions regarding the disciples	10:1-16	3:13-19	9:1
		6:7,13	

not want otherwise lying spirits to testify to the truth. Only once did Jesus ask them to identify themselves (Mark 5:9). Jesus wanted Israel to believe the truth because it came from the mouth of *God* and not from the mouth of *demons*. Also, He did not want to give the people weighing the evidence of His deliverance an opportunity to reject Him because testimony came from an unreliable source.

Jesus' unique ministry is seen again in the third general statement of casting out demons. This incident involved John the Baptist, who had been put into prison by King Herod because he offended Herod's wife with his preaching. While in prison John began to wonder if Jesus was really the Messiah after all. He sent a messenger to Jesus to inquire about the matter, and Jesus' response is described in Luke 7:21: "At that very time He cured many people of diseases and afflictions and evil spirits." This description of what Jesus was doing was enough to remove all doubt from John, because it was a description of indisputable messianic activity.

The Specific Cases

The seven specific incidents described in the first three Gospels follow the general pattern which we observed above. In the first incident Jesus entered a synagogue, a place of worship, and an unclean spirit cried out of someone, "What do we have to do with You, Jesus of Nazareth? Have You come to destroy us? I know who You are—the Holy One of God!" (Mark 1:24). Once again Jesus commanded the demon to be quiet and then cast the evil spirit out of the man. This incident brought Jesus notoriety regarding His authority over the demonic.

Without a doubt the most extensive narrative relating to the demonic occurs in the incident often entitled "The Gadarene Demoniac" (Mark 5:1-20). This is the story about Jesus casting demons out of a man and into a herd of swine. As usual, the encounter began when the demons in the man recognized Christ as "Jesus, Son of the Most High God" (Mark 5:7). Jesus then cast out the demons, but here He commanded the unclean spirit to first give Him his name. The demon replied, "My name is Legion, for we are many" (Mark 5:9). Notice that the demon was not named lust, gossip, adultery, hate, or any of the other names often given by demons to those involved in contemporary deliverance attempts. "Legion" is more of a generic description which shows that there were many unclean spirits within the man. It could not have been a proper name unless the entire multitude all had the same name—a highly unlikely possibility. Instead of the current popular belief that names of demons are related to the sin or habit which they inflict upon their subject, the Bible reveals something quite different.

This is the only place where Jesus carried on a dialogue with demons, but it was not to get information from them, as some contemporary deliverance practices advocate, but rather to accommodate a request from the demons as to where they would be going. When the man was delivered, Jesus forbade him to travel with Him, but instead instructed him to return "home to your people and report to them what great things the Lord has done for you, and how He had mercy on you" (Mark 5:19). Christ did not allow the demons to testify to who He was, but He did want this delivered man to testify to God's mercy, which was the basis for his deliverance.

Incidents three through seven follow the same general pattern as noted in the previous examples.

One of the most significant observations we can make is that *not a single one of these cases reveals someone who came to Jesus in order to be delivered of a demon*! Each person was brought by someone else, except for the Gadarene. And in that instance he did not come to Jesus to be delivered, but "he ran up and bowed down," indicating worship, and asked, "What do I have to do with You, Jesus, Son of the Most High God?" Then he begged Jesus not to torment him. This man clearly was not coming for deliverance. If anything can be inferred from these examples, it is that demon-possessed people do not seek deliverance.

The Disciples and the Demons

The twelve disciples of Jesus became involved in casting out demons when Jesus sent them out to declare to their fellow Israelites that the kingdom of God was at hand. Mark seems to indicate that this commissioning occurred twice, in 3:13-19 and 6:7-13. Clearly the reason why Christ gave His disciples this power and authority over the demonic realm was as an authenticating sign to their fellow countrymen that their Rabbi was indeed the Messiah, because only Messiah could truly deliver those under the domain of the demonic. This was a power and authority given only to the twelve disciples, and lest there be any misunderstanding who they were, they were specifically named in Matthew 10:2-4. Jesus instructed them, "As you go, preach, saying, 'The kingdom of heaven is at hand.' Heal the sick, raise the dead, cleanse the lepers, cast out demons" (Matthew 10:7,8). Just like the ministry of Christ, so the ministry of the twelve disciples in relation to casting out demons was a sign pointing to the coming of the messianic kingdom.

All of this evidence that Jesus was the Messiah led to a head-on collision with the Jewish leaders of Christ's day. They feared that they would lose their positions of leadership if Jesus really was the Messiah. So when they were backed into a corner, having to admit the genuine messianic quality of the miracles and demonic deliverance which Jesus demonstrated, they tried to say that the source of His power and authority came not from God, but from a deal which Jesus worked out with Satan himself so that He could put on a good show.

The Point Is Clear

The central role of Jesus' demonstration of His power and authority over Satan and the demonic comes center stage in the drama of the Gospels. One particular incident was triggered by Jesus' deliverance of a demon-possessed man (Matthew 12:22). The response of the people was that of amazement as they wondered, "This man cannot be the Son of David, can he?" (Matthew 12:23). When the scribes and Pharisees heard this, they accused Jesus of being in league with Satan himself. Christ refuted them personally first, then went on to refute the logic of their charge, showing it to be false. The point is clear: Jesus' rule over Satan and the demonic was a sign that He was Messiah, since only Messiah would be stronger than Satan.

— 7 —

STRATEGIES OF THE ENEMY

When the unclean spirit goes out of a man, it passes through waterless places seeking rest, and not finding any it says, "I will return to my house from which I came." And when it comes, it finds it swept and put in order. Then it goes and takes along seven other spirits more evil than itself, and they go in and live there; and the last state of that man becomes worse than the first.

—Luke 11:24-26

Tonight was the night that several of us had been waiting for all week. The evangelist was going to hold a deliverance service on the final night of a week of meetings. This "deliverance minister" had been teaching us all week about Satan and the demonic, and now the time had finally arrived to see him practice what he had preached.

Our carload of Christians focused our discussion on Jane as we expectantly drove to the other side of town. Jane had come to believe that the demon of gossip resided in her after hearing the teaching that week. We were all trying to discern, on the basis of what we had been learning, if Jane spent six to eight hours a day on the phone gossiping because she had a demon or, as her husband thought, because it was just her personality. Jane decided she would go forward to be delivered from a demon that she was convinced was the root of her problem.

As we pulled into the parking lot, we saw that this night was going to see the largest crowd of the week. We made our way to the pew that we had occupied all week and sat down anticipating the action. We were not disappointed. During the course of that evening we saw some truly amazing things. Some of the incidents included a lady who had multiple voices shrieking out of her. Another lady keeled over with convulsions when the minister commanded the demon to depart in the name of Jesus. A young boy passed out and swooned on the floor for a long time. Another lady literally vomited up what the minister called the demon of gluttony in response to the evangelist's command to that evil spirit to leave. Virtually every case handled by the deliverance minister was bizarre and seemed to require his vast experience and discernment to finally see through the bag of tricks implemented by the demons in their always-futile effort to continue the demonization of their subject.

Jane made it to the front as 9:00 approached that evening. The evangelist motioned to her that she would be next. He rapidly began his interrogation of Jane in the style which had preceded the deliverance of the others. "Are you a Christian?" "Yes." "Have you renounced all of the works of Satan from your past?" "Yes," she proclaimed. "Then what is the nature of your oppression?" he asked in an effort to find the basis of her plight. Jane then confessed her excessive participation in gossip. She renounced it in the name of Jesus as the minister ordered the demon to manifest himself. When the evil spirit finally spoke, the minister demanded to know the demon's name. "Chatter!" the voice screamed back. "I love to talk about other people!" "Well, your use of this child of God's vocal cords is about to cease, because I am sending you to the pit," proclaimed the minister. He then commanded the demon to leave Jane in the name of Jesus as he "pled the blood" over his subject. The demon let out a sudden, high-pitched screech which startled most of us in the room, and then departed. Jane returned to her seat having apparently gained victory over Satan.

Time ran out shortly after Jane's deliverance, so the evangelist had all of those raise their hands who believed that they had some kind of demonic oppression. Almost every hand in the place shot into the air. He then led them through a group deliverance and gave a few parting words on how to keep delivered and not return to the bondage of demonic oppression.

Deliverance Expert?

I recall the next few months; every time I (Thomas) had any kind of problem in my life I instantly believed that it was some kind of demonic oppression. I would go through the steps which we had learned at the meeting for casting out demons, just in case they were still there.

My friend Jane quickly developed into our local deliverance expert, and spent much time on the telephone repeatedly casting out demons from our friends anytime they encountered the slightest problem. Jane's life went from one crisis experience to another. Her husband was transferred out of town a few months later, and about a year after that I heard that they were experiencing severe marital problems, which eventually led to divorce. After that I never heard from either of them again.

I was a young Christian when I went through this exposure to contemporary deliverance teaching and practice (about 20 years ago). After years of studying the Scriptures I have become convinced that this kind of teaching and practice is really not found in the Bible. As I look back on what I went through then and see this same kind of approach to Satan and the demonic growing by leaps and bounds in our own day, a number of questions repeatedly come to mind. How much control does God allow Satan to have over people? More specifically, what can Satan do and not do to believers? However, the most provocative question of them all, which neither the deliverance minister, myself, nor my friends brought up for discussion at that time, was whether a true, born-again believer could even be demon-possessed. If Christians cannot be demon-possessed, then the whole notion of a believers' deliverance ministry is not scripturally valid. If a Christian *can* be demonized, then a whole different scenario would follow for spiritual warfare. It is time to deal with these questions, starting with how much control Satan has over people.

The Power of God

The book of Job is considered by many Bible scholars to have been the first book of the Bible given to man from God. At the beginning of the story, when the angels (holy and unholy) came to present themselves before the Lord, He said to Satan, "From where do you come?" Satan answered, "From roaming about on the earth and walking around on it" (Job 1:7). Why was Satan "cruising" the earth? A similar expression is found in 1 Peter 5:8, where Peter says that "your adversary, the devil, prowls about like a roaring lion, seeking someone to devour." The answer is clear: Satan roams and walks around the earth in order to find someone whom he can devour. However, as we continue to follow the development of Satan's dialogue with the Lord, we find that even though the evil one is *capable* of attacking human beings, this does not mean that he is *permitted* to.

A major emphasis in the book of Job is the sovereignty of God. We need to recognize that nothing happens in God's creation without God's permission, including evil. God is not the author of sin, but His plan for His creation allowed for man's choice and the presence of evil.

Satan and mankind are responsible for introducing and maintaining sin in God's world. In spite of this, God is still sovereign over the evil which happened to Job.

First, God appears to have had a regular time in which all the angels, both elect and evil, had to report to Him (Job 1:6; 2:1). This is an indication that He rules over both domains. Second, the Lord initiated the conversation with Satan by asking him if he had "considered My servant Job." Third, Satan then asked permission from the Lord to harm Job. Surely Satan would not be asking permission on a matter like this if it were not necessary! Fourth, Satan recognized that the Lord had put a hedge (fence) around Job and his house which prevented Satan from stalking Job without God's permission. Fifth, after the Lord granted Satan permission, He limited the extent of suffering which Satan would be permitted to inflict (Job 1:12; 2:6).

God's sovereignty over His creation means that Satan does not have a free hand to run roughshod over God's creatures, especially His children, without the Lord's permission. The psalmist says, "Surely the wrath of man shall praise thee: the remainder of wrath shalt thou restrain" (Psalm 76:10 KJV). The interaction between God and Satan in Job illustrates this. However, some people advocate the view that we have to "pray a hedge of thorns" around fellow believers in order to protect them. The Scriptures indicate that God automatically erects a hedge of thorns around His children. Like any loving Father, God moves to protect His family members from the moment of salvation.

God's sovereignty over *all* of His creation needs to be kept in mind if we are to avoid two common errors. First, when people learn about the things which Satan can do, they sometimes respond as if God does not restrain Satan's activity. Some people say they know that God is sovereign but then fail to apply that aspect of His character by acting as if it were all up to them to protect themselves from Satan's attacks. Once again, they admit in *theory* that God is sovereign, but they *behave* in a way which actually denies His sovereignty. Those who are especially vulnerable to this incorrect perception are constantly worried about whether or not they may have some unknown sin, curse, or family heritage from the past with which they have not specifically dealt and which could be the basis for a "satanic stronghold." This error is a failure to realize that God sovereignly applied all aspects of His salvation to our lives when we became His children.

Second, if God's sovereignty is not taken into account as we study what Satan can do to people, then we may react to this information in a fatalistic way. Knowledge of the many ways in which Satan can attack people could cause us to merely throw up our hands in surrender and say, "What's the use of trying to battle against impossible odds?" This is the flip side of the first error. The properly-oriented believer should respond with an active trust in God which is characterized by a quiet confidence in God's protection.

God's sovereignty is like a filter which protects us from anything which He has not planned to bring into our lives to mold us into the image of our model—Jesus Christ. Now that we have our filters snugly fitted, we will look at what Satan does to people.

Satan's Subordinate Power

Satan and demons can affect people in many ways. Yet just because they have this capacity does not mean that all of the things we will list happen with the same frequency or to all people, or even that they are necessarily demonic in origin in a particular case. We are pointing out the things which Satan *is capable of* and has done *at one time or another.*

We have already seen that Satan is the opponent of God, which explains why all of his activity is aimed at distorting what God has made. Jesus makes this point in John 10:10: "The thief comes only to steal, and kill, and destroy; I came that they might have life, and might have it abundantly." Jesus creates something, but Satan destroys it.

If God has given us a gift, Satan wants to steal it. God has given us life, but Satan wants to bring death. If God has built or created something, Satan wants to smash and destroy it. God gave Adam and Eve the gift of a beautiful life in Eden, but Satan said that God was still holding back something good. When the first couple fell for that lie, they lost the gift of Eden and were cast into a wilderness as a result.

God has given to each person life, both physically and spiritually. Satan often attempts to persuade people that death is to be preferred over life. This may take many forms. He may encourage one person to take the life of a fellow human being, as Cain did to Abel. Or he may try to convince a person that the only way out of his problems is to take his own life—to commit suicide, as King Saul did. Or he may use a worldly way of thinking to try to convince a woman that she would make a wise choice if she got an abortion or to persuade a man that he could be happy only if he left his wife and four children. But Christ came to give life back to fallen man through salvation, as well as to teach us how to live a lifestyle which is called often in Proverbs "the way of life." Proverbs 15:4 tells us that what we say now affects the quality of life we live now: "A soothing tongue is a tree of life, but perversion in it crushes the spirit."

God is the One who created the marvelous world in which we live. Satan, on the other hand, is constantly trying to destroy the work of God. Satan loves to destroy relationships such as marriage and the family. Satan is like the malicious little child who breaks everything he can get his hands on.

Satan wants to destroy and pervert our relationship with and worship of God by promoting idolatry and false religion. He does this by distorting who Jesus really is, by making people feel good about their false worship and idolatry, and by teaching that we can achieve salvation through doing good works. Satan and his demons are the source of false doctrine. Paul called this kind of deception "doctrines of demons" produced by "deceitful spirits" (1 Timothy 4:1).

Satan's Other Powers

Satan also has an impact upon nations. Daniel 10:13 records the incident of a heavenly struggle, lasting three weeks, between an elect angel and the "prince of the kingdom of Persia," representing the demonic realm. It became necessary for the elect angel to gain the assistance of a higher-ranking angel, Michael, because he could not handle the prince of Persia alone. This event took place in relation to God's revelation of His plan for Israel and the Gentile nations. Therefore this "angelic conflict" affects the affairs of nations upon earth. Revelation 16:13-16 is an example of a similar effect that demons will have in influencing the plans and actions of leaders during the tribulation. Possibly the rapid changes that have taken place in Eastern Europe have been the result of an angelic conflict.

These passages have been used by some to develop the doctrine referred to as "territorial spirits." At the root of this teaching is an element of truth—the truth that demons do indeed exercise a certain geopolitical influence, according to Scripture. However, this is all that Scripture says about the subject. The vast majority of what is said today about territorial spirits is developed from experience, not the Bible.

There is no indication in the Scriptures that believers are to pray away the influence of these demons or that it is necessary to free a city, neighborhood, or nation from the influence of these demons in order to reach the inhabitants with the gospel. Once again this approach reflects a "devil made me do it" approach. Advocates of this doctrine assume that the reason people in a given area fail to respond to the gospel is because they are being kept from it by demons. But Scripture never presents the problem in this way. While it is true that all unsaved people are being blinded by Satan (2 Corinthians 4:4), there is no example or command in Scripture urging us to pray away these demons before there can be a gospel impact. Paul and his associates certainly never reflected this approach in the book of Acts. This idea is really based on too low a view of God's power and too high a view of Satan's power.

Besides blinding people to the gospel, Satan and his demons may also inflict physical disease and even death upon people. This is illustrated in the first two chapters of Job, where the Lord gives Satan permission to harm Job with physical sickness and then to kill his children. Some of the physical diseases listed in the Bible which might have a demonic source include epilepsy (Matthew 17:15-18), dumbness (Matthew 9:33), blindness (Matthew 17:15-18), deafness (Mark 9:25), and physical deformity (Luke 13:11,16).

Some mental disorders may also be caused by the demons (Mark 5:4,5). Such bizarre behavior may include violence (Matthew 8:28), outbursts of abnormal strength (Mark 5:4), raving/crying/screaming (Mark 5:5), self-mutilation (Mark 5:5), foaming at the mouth (Mark 9:20), nakedness (Luke 8:27), and grinding of teeth (Mark 9:18).

It is absolutely imperative to state that *these conditions are not always caused by demons*. In addition, not every bona fide demon-possession has identical effects. Today many people may make the incorrect mental leap that a violent person must be demon-possessed simply because that can sometimes be one of the characteristics of demon-possession. Moreover, even when the ultimate cause of the disease or problem is supernatural, the biblical solution does not necessarily lie in a direct engagement with the demon. Scripture always presents the solution in terms of *prayer and obedience to God*. More will be said about this in the next chapter.

What happens when a person accepts Jesus Christ as his Savior and becomes a Christian? In what way does this impact how Satan and his demons can affect that person?

What Is Demon-Possession?

How does the Bible describe and define demon-possession? In order to properly understand the biblical teaching about spiritual warfare, we must start with a clear understanding of what Scripture means when it refers to demon-possession. A wrong perspective on this matter will result in misunderstanding God's Word as He has spoken it, causing us to rely instead on human opinion.

Since there is no clear example of demon-possession in the Old Testament, our examination will concentrate on the New Testament. The New Testament uses more than one term to refer to demon-possession. First is the Greek word *daimonizomai*, which is a participial form of the more commonly used noun for demon (*daimonion*). *Daimonizomai* is usually translated "to be possessed by a demon," or when it is used to describe a person in that condition it is rendered "demoniac." The word is used 13 times,[1] all in the Gospels, and is usually referred to by the English expression "to be demonized."

The second term in the Greek is *daimonion echein*, "to have a demon." This phrase is used eight times in Matthew, Luke, and John.[2] The Greek grammar conveys the idea that the subject is characterized by having a demon indwell him.

A classic definition often quoted is one given by the late Merrill Unger:

> Demon possession is a condition in which one or more evil spirits or demons inhabit the body of a human being and can take complete control of their victim at will. By temporarily blotting out his consciousness, they can speak and act through him as their complete slave and tool. The inhabiting demon (or demons) comes and goes much like the proprietor of a house who may or may not be "at home." When the demon is "at home," he may precipitate an attack. In these attacks the victim passes from his normal state, in which he acts like other people, to the abnormal state of possession.[3]

So far this is a fairly good definition; however, as Unger later develops his definition it becomes apparent that he is relying, at least to some degree, on experiences with what he believed to be demonically possessed people.

---

1. Matthew 4:24; 8:16,28,33; 9:32; 12:22; 15:22; Mark 1:32; 5:15,16,18; Luke 8:36; John 10:21.
2. Matthew 11:18; Luke 7:33; 8:27; John 7:20; 8:48,49 ("to not have a demon"), 52; 10:20.
3. Merrill F. Unger, *Demons in the World Today* (Wheaton: Tyndale House Publishers, 1971), p. 102.

Extrabiblical Jumble

We believe that a sound definition of demonization must be based solely on the information in the Bible. Unfortunately some today let experience determine even more of the definition:

> The difficulty with Dr. Unger's definition is that although it may be correct in some cases, it may not be broad enough to function in all cases of demonization.[4]

This writer, like many others, is developing his own autonomous definition of demon-possession based on human experience and then reading it back into the Bible. It is this type of invalid methodology which usually leads people to the conclusion that Christians can be demon-possessed.

Once a person moves beyond Scripture as his authority, anything becomes possible if carried to further extremes. (And there always seem to be some people who are willing to push an idea further than the contemporary consensus.) The following list reveals what people in the seventeenth century believed to be symptoms of a demon-possessed person:

> a) to think oneself possessed, b) to lead a wicked life, c) to be persistently ill, falling into heavy sleep and vomiting unusual objects (either natural objects: toads, serpents, worms, iron, stones, etc.; or artificial objects: nails, pins, etc.), d) to blaspheme, e) to make a pact with the Devil, f) to be troubled with spirits, g) to show a frightening and horrible countenance, h) to be tired of living, i) to be uncontrollable and violent, j) to make sounds and movements like an animal.[5]

If we allow any basis at all for extrabiblical thought on this matter, it can open up a floodgate of errant thought. For example, who could

---

4. John Wimber, *Spiritual Warfare* (Anaheim, CA: Mercy Publishing/Vineyard Ministries International, 1989), p. 98.
5. Cited by Willem Berends, "The Biblical Criteria for Demon-Possession," in *The Westminister Theological Journal*, XXXVII:3, Spring 1975 (Westminister Theological Seminary) p. 342; from R. H. Robbins, *The Encyclopedia of Witchcraft and Demonology* (New York: Crown Publishers, 1959), p. 395.

say that the above seventeenth-century list is wrong if the Bible alone is not the standard? Everyone's opinion becomes just as possible as anyone else's. Let's see how the Bible *alone* describes demon-possession.

The True Picture

Since no systematic definition is given in the Bible of demon-possession, the best way to understand this issue is to look at the characteristics of demonization in the biblical examples. We see from the two basic terms noted above that someone who is said to be "demonized" or "to have a demon" is a person who has one or more demons dwelling *within* him. For example, while the Gadarene demoniac is labeled as "demonized" in Mark 5:15,16,18, he is said to "have a demon" in Luke 8:27. A variation of this synonymous usage occurs when demon-possessed people are said to "have an unclean spirit" (Mark 5:2,8) or are described by a similar term. A popular approach today is to say that the idea of demon-possession per se is not in the Greek of the New Testament:

> To be demonized means to be under the control of one or more demons. Demonization is not a matter of extremes, such as the either/or idea of being completely free or totally bound; it's a matter of degrees.[6]

This approach commits the fallacy of defining a word based on its root meanings, or etymology, rather than on how the word is actually used. "Demonized" and "to have a demon" are used in Scripture of only one extreme: to be inwardly controlled by an indwelling demon. They are never used to describe a case involving anything less. For example, these terms never describe Satan's activities of accusation, temptation, deception, or persecution; they describe only the extreme case of being inwardly controlled by a demon.

Jesus gives us a picture of demon-possession in one of His dialogues with the Pharisees. In Matthew 12:28,29, 43-45 Jesus pictures the possessed victim as a house in which demons dwell. Casting out the demons is analogous to throwing the inhabitants out of the house. Therefore it is clear that demon-possession includes evil/unclean

6. Neil T. Anderson, *The Bondage Breaker* (Eugene, OR: Harvest House, 1990), p. 174.

spirits, another term for demons, indwelling an individual. This is further reinforced by the terms used to describe the moving in and eviction of demons from their captive. Both transitions are recorded in Mark 5:13, with the "coming out" of the demons from their human hostage as they then "entered into" the herd of swine. Mary Magdalene is described in Luke 8:2 as the woman "from whom seven demons had gone out."

Dr. Unger's definition cited above is a good description of how, once inside a person, demons can then "speak and act through him as their complete slave and tool.... When the demon is 'at home,' he may precipitate an attack. In these attacks the victim passes from his normal state, in which he acts like other people, to the abnormal state of possession."[7]

Biblical demon-possession is the direct, inward control of demons (also called evil spirits) of their victim by residing in him. We will now examine the crucial issue of whether or not Christians can be demon-possessed. Can this happen to Christians?

Can a Christian Be Demon-Possessed?

We do not believe that the Bible teaches that a Christian can be possessed or indwelt by a demon. We *do* believe, however, that Christians can be severely influenced or oppressed by Satan and the demonic. The key issues on this matter revolve around the differences between *internal* control/inhabitation and *external* influence.

Scripture clearly teaches that the Holy Spirit indwells each believer. First Corinthians 6:19 says, "Do you not know that your body is a temple of the Holy Spirit who is in you, whom you have from God?" The Holy Spirit lives inside everyone who knows Christ. He dwells in their house. In addition, 1 John 4:4 tells us, "Greater is He who is in you [the Holy Spirit] than he who is in the world [Satan and the demonic]." Therefore a demon is not able to enter and take control of a believer because the Holy Spirit lives there. We could picture it this way: Since the Holy Spirit lives in the house of a believer, then every time a demon knocks at the door the Holy Spirit answers. Since God the Holy Spirit is stronger than any demonic being, including Satan himself, then no demon or evil spirit could enter. It's that simple: God is greater than Satan, and thus He protects His children.

---

7. Unger, *Demons*, p. 102.

But is this a nat'l anecdote?

In the example Christ cited to the Pharisees in Matthew 12:43 ("When the unclean spirit goes out of a man, it passes through waterless places, seeking rest, and does not find it"), the demon is searching for a new home because he was cast out of the individual he once occupied. Then the homeless demon says, "I will return to my house from which I came" (verse 44). The demon and his friends can only enter the house if it is empty—unoccupied. In the case of all believers the house is *occupied,* and God the Holy Spirit answers the door even if repossession is attempted. This passage is saying that only *empty* houses—unbelievers—can be reoccupied. Therefore Christians cannot be demon-possessed.

Several other New Testament passages indicate that Christ's victory over Satan and the demonic was so great that he cannot come back and repossess believers. Jesus prayed in His great high-priestly prayer that the Father "keep them [Christians] from the evil one" (John 17:15). We know that the Father has heard and is fulfilling Christ's request. The apostle John later wrote that each believer is kept by God and that "the evil one does not touch him" (1 John 5:18). It is hard to imagine how a believer could be demon-possessed but also be said to have not been touched by the evil one! Certainly this passage would add weight to the teaching that believers cannot be demon-possessed.

Paul declared in 2 Thessalonians 3:3 that "the Lord is faithful, and He will strengthen and protect you from the evil one." This protection is based upon the Lord's faithfulness. It is hard to believe that our faithful Lord's protection would allow one of His children to become demon-possessed. It doesn't make sense in the light of Scripture. Why then do some assert that believers can be open to some form of demonic possession?

Contemporary Arguments

A popular approach today is to say that the Christians can be demon-possessed on the basis of case studies. C. Fred Dickason is typical of some who conclude that Christians can be demon-possessed. He states that the biblical data are inconclusive: "From the survey and analysis for arguments pro and con, we conclude that we cannot say with reasonable certainty that either position is correct."[8] How

8. C. Fred Dickason, *Demon Possession and the Christian: A New Perspective* (Chicago: Moody Press, 1987), p. 147.

does he seek to resolve this alleged tie? He enters into the realm of "scientific investigation." After citing many case studies from reputable sources he concludes, "We must allow the distinct probability that biblically guided investigation and counsel has shown in experience that some Christians have been demonized. The evidence is heavily weighted toward that conclusion."[9] Apparently he is not able to interpret the Bible in a decisive way on this issue, but he is able to analyze and interpret human experience outside the realm of Scripture in such a way that the scales are tipped in favor of Christian demon-possession. Dickason's interpretation of these case studies leads him to declare that the "burden of proof lies with those who deny that Christians can be demonized."[10] Why? In a tie, no burden is assessed on either side. But we think Scripture is clear, as we have already shown.

Like many who have struggled to answer this question, Merrill Unger changed his view, although the change was not a result of further Bible study and improved biblical insight on the matter. He shifted away from the statement "To demon possession only unbelievers are exposed"[11] to the statement "Demon influence may occur in different degrees of severity and in a variety of forms, both in Christians and non-Christians."[12] What changed Unger's mind? As with Dickason, it was the experiences of Christians. Unger wrote, "Since the first publication of *Biblical Demonology* in 1952, the author has received many letters from missionaries all over the world who question the theory that true believers cannot be demon-possessed.... The claims of these missionaries appear valid."[13]

To summarize this position, we see Dickason and Unger saying that the Scriptures do not discuss the issue of demon-possession in enough detail for us to determine whether believers can be demon-possessed, so with this cloud of uncertainty we must enter a different arena to decide the issue—the arena of experience. This experiential evidence is so great that we must break the tie in favor of the concept that Christians can be demon-possessed.

However, this approach has some serious problems.

---

9. Dickason, *Demon Possession*, p. 186.
10. Ibid., p. 175.
11. Merrill F. Unger, *Biblical Demonology* (Wheaton: Scripture Press Publications, 1952), p. 100.
12. Unger, *Demons*, p. 113.
13. Ibid., p. 117.

Back to the Source

First, the whole idea that any area of thought is removed from the divine-viewpoint authority of Scripture is a fallacy. Scripture is to be the source from which we derive a biblical framework so that we can then enter the other fields of thought in order to extend our learning and develop wisdom. Without definite conclusions from the Bible to guide us in the unseen spiritual realm of the demonic, we are no different from someone trying to explore Carlsbad Caverns in the dark. When we do this we have in effect abandoned God's Word in this area and substituted our own thoughts and experiences, instead of interpreting our experiences within the light of the Bible. Jesus told Nicodemus in John 3 that He descended from heaven specifically for the purpose of revealing heavenly things (verses 9-13), which we earthbound creatures cannot discover at all if God does not tell us. So case studies and experience are not the way to break the alleged tie found in Scripture.

Second, Dickason so loosely interprets the biblical data for why a Christian cannot be demon-possessed that he naturally concludes that the Bible is not clear. Because he believes there are valid arguments which indicate that a believer can be demon-possessed, he is forced to declare that the Bible is totally inconclusive on this subject. The fact that the Trinity indwells and protects the believer should be reason enough for anyone to conclude that Christians cannot be demon-possessed. Furthermore, when this truth is combined with the fact that demon-possession is not even mentioned as something believers should be concerned about after the resurrection of Christ and the coming of the Holy Spirit on the day of Pentecost, then it should remove any doubt that might still be lingering. The burden of proof lies with those who believe that Christians can be demon-possessed, since the Scriptures do not support that point of view. Valid proof must flow from the Scriptures, not from experience.

Dickason and others go to great lengths in their tapes and books to show from their case studies that the Christians they counseled were under such great demonic bondage that only a diagnosis of demon-possession accounts for their symptoms. Often the believer is pictured as having tried all the techniques of the Christian life as found in the New Testament, but without success in dealing with his or her problem. The point which is often emphasized is that if the person had not realized that he was demon-possessed and been delivered, he would not have had the means to overcome his problem by applying the God-given principles found in the Bible.

But if Christians can be possessed, then why do not the New Testament Epistles, those letters written specifically to teach believers how to live a victorious Christian life until the return of Christ, tell us that believers can be demon-possessed, or command us to cast out demons from Christians, or tell us how to otherwise deal with this problem? It is unthinkable that a subject as important as this one would not be dealt with in the Epistles.

The Voice of Silence

If Scripture is not clear as to whether Christians can be demon-possessed, then it cannot be clear as to how to deal with Christians who are demon-possessed. Conversely, if the Epistles gave instructions on how to cast out demons, then it would be clear that Christians could be demon-possessed. Therefore, since there are no instructions for dealing with demon-possessed Christians in the New Testament, and assuming that believers can be demon-possessed, then once again it is back to experience and trial-and-error as our teacher for functioning in this area.

To those who suggest that some of our arguments are based on the silence of Scripture, we believe that such silence speaks volumes. In Chapter 2 we showed that the Bible clearly claims to give us *everything pertaining to life and godliness* (2 Peter 1:3) and is *adequate to equip us for every good work* (2 Timothy 3:17). Christian demon-possession is certainly a vital matter pertaining to godliness for which we should be equipped. If the Bible claims to give *everything* pertaining to godliness but ignores this particular subject, we can be absolutely confident that Christians need not worry about demon-possession. Therefore those who teach Christian possession are by implication denying the sufficiency of Scripture and are going beyond its authority by promoting their own. They have forgotten the warning of Paul: "...that in us you might learn not to exceed what is written, in order that no one of you might become arrogant in behalf of one against the other" (1 Corinthians 4:6).

Merrill Unger in his earlier book, *Biblical Demonology*, made the following helpful observation:

> To demon possession only unbelievers are exposed; to demon influence, both believers and unbelievers. In the one case, the personality is actually invaded, the body inhabited, and a dominating control is gained; while in the other

> instance, attack is made from without, through pressure, suggestion, and temptation.[14]

This statement accurately expresses our own view and properly distinguishes the demonic impact upon unbelievers and believers. The major characteristic of *possession* is an internal assault upon the unbeliever. Demonic *influence* upon believers is an assault from without. The difference is as great as having an enemy *within* your house who has a gun pointed at your head making you obey his wishes versus having someone *outside* who is trying to persuade you to do something. As Unger noted, demonic influence from without takes the form of persuasion "through pressure, suggestion, and temptation." The believer, therefore, is not under the type of bondage which those who believe that a Christian can be demon-possessed often imagine. Instead, the will has been freed by Christ to obey, although the believer may choose to submit to Satan rather than Christ in a given instance. On the other hand, if he were truly demonized he would have to be delivered before he could be free to obey.

Some Christians make a similar distinction between possession and influence in theory but then define what they mean by "influence" in such a way that for all practical purposes they are saying that a believer can be demon-possessed. We have heard one version of that view go something like this: "Demon-possession really means demonization in the New Testament. A Christian cannot be demon-possessed but he can be demonized." (As we saw earlier, to be demon-possessed is to be demonized and vice versa.) This view then describes "influence" upon believers in such a way that it is really the type of internal *possession* which affects unbelievers.

The Refutable Examples

"Satan can and does demonize believers,"[15] declares John Wimber. Wimber attempts to support his belief that Christians can be demon-possessed from several biblical passages. His first example is King Saul, whose story is told in the book of 1 Samuel. We agree with Wimber that Saul was a believer. However, Wimber wrongly equates the fact that Saul was tormented (16:14) with demon-possession.

---

14. Unger, *Demonology*, p. 100.
15. Wimber, *Warfare*, p. 100.

For several reasons this could not have been a true case of demon-possession. 1) The evil spirit is said to have been sent from God, not Satan (16:14). 2) The evil spirit would leave when David played his harp (16:23), and no demon is said in Scripture to depart at the playing of music. Instead, demons are cast out in the name of the Lord. 3) Saul later repented of his sin (26:21). The New Testament presents a demon-possessed person as a victim who needs freedom, not repentance. 4) The Hebrew text says that the evil spirit would come *upon* Saul or depart from *upon* him; it is never said to have entered *into* Saul, as would be expected if demon-possession was the intended idea. We saw earlier that the language of demon-possession is that of *entering into* and *exiting out of* a person, not coming upon. The description in this passage is consistent with an external attack which does happen to believers. Finally, since the case of King Saul is considered the strongest candidate for demon-possession in the Old Testament, it follows that there are no genuine cases of demon-possession recorded in the Old Testament.

Wimber cites Luke 13:16 and the fact that Jesus called a woman who had been demon-possessed for 18 years "a daughter of Abraham." Wimber thinks that this means she was a believer. First, he has not proved from this that a New Testament believer can be demon-possessed, especially a post-pentecost Christian. Second, "daughter of Abraham" is very likely a nationalist term for a female citizen of Israel. Many Israelites were believers, but most were not. Nothing in the text indicates whether she was at that time a believer.

Judas, according to Wimber, was a believer because he was one of the twelve disciples. There is no question that Judas was demon-possessed. John 13:27 uses clear "demon-possession" language in describing the fact that "Satan then entered into him [Judas]." It should be equally clear, however, that Judas was *not* a believer. First, Jesus commented in John 6:70, "Did I Myself not choose you, the twelve, and yet one of you is a devil?" Judas is singled out as that devil in the next verse. This is hardly a term for a Christian. Certainly the burden of proof would be on someone to prove that Judas was a believer after a comment like that on his resume. Second, Jesus said in John 13:10-11 that all the twelve disciples were "clean" (to have one's sins forgiven) *except Judas*. It is wrong to equate a disciple as necessarily being a believer, since not all of Christ's disciples were believers.

Peter is said by Wimber to have been demon-possessed when he was rebuked by Jesus in Matthew 16:23. Once again, this is an inferential assumption which can be demonstrated to be wrong. Satan's influence was that of persuasion from without, not an operation from within. Why? Because Peter had accepted a wrong view about the role of Messiah: Peter did not want Jesus to die. But this was contrary to God's will for Jesus, so Jesus rebuked Peter to let him know the source of that type of false thinking. Earlier, when Peter had declared that Jesus was "the Christ, the Son of the living God" (16:16), Jesus had said that the source and inspiration of *that* thought was a revelation from God. However, when Peter rebuked Jesus for following the revelation of God's will for His life, Jesus wanted to make sure that Peter knew that the source of this thinking was not *God* but *Satan*. Notice that Jesus explained after His rebuke that Peter was not setting his "mind on God's interests, but man's" (16:23). This is a picture of Satan using persuasion from outside Peter to try to convince him to believe false teaching.

Wimber contends that Ananias and Sapphira were believers who were demonized to lie because "Satan *filled* your heart to lie to the Holy Spirit" (Acts 5:3). Surely someone whose heart is "filled" with something is experiencing internal control and thus demon-possession, Wimber would contend. We will not debate whether Ananias and Sapphira were believers, but will assume that they were. The difficulty with this verse is that so little information is given. It is possible to understand the phrase "Satan filled your heart" in two ways. The first is that Satan, the "father of lies" (John 8:44), influenced the heart of Ananias to lie. This would be similar to the type of external, mental persuasion that we saw in the previous event involving Peter. The second way, the way Wimber takes it, is that Satan himself filled the heart of Ananias. However, if this were the case, then it would be Satan who lied; yet it was *Ananias* who lied and was punished. Had Ananias been Satan- or demon-possessed, it would have been Satan inside him who was lying, and the solution would have been to cast out Satan, since Ananias would be the innocent victim and not the perpetrator which the Bible declares him to have been. The next verse says, "Why is it that you have conceived this deed in your heart?" (Acts 5:4). Ananias is in control and responsible for his action, not Satan. Since the passage gives no clear indication that Ananias was indwelt by Satan, it is best to see this as an example of Satan using the rebellious heart of a Christian as a base of operations. Would possession relieve one of responsibility?

Wimber believes that the man in 1 Corinthians 5 was a believer whose behavior was a symptom of demon-possession, and that Paul placed this man out of the church and into the sphere of Satan for discipline, with the result that the man could lose his physical life, even though this would not affect his eternal destiny (verse 5). However, Satan does not have to possess a person to kill him. King Saul was not demon-possessed, but he was driven to death by an evil spirit (1 Samuel 31). Job was certainly in no danger of being demon-possessed, but the Lord told Satan that he could do anything to him except kill him. Paul was given a thorn in the flesh to buffet him, a demonic messenger (2 Corinthians 12:7), yet he was not demon-possessed.

The Intensity Line

When answering this important question of demon-possession of Christians, especially in the light of various experiences which seem to indicate demonic possession of Christians, we find it helpful to use this chart.

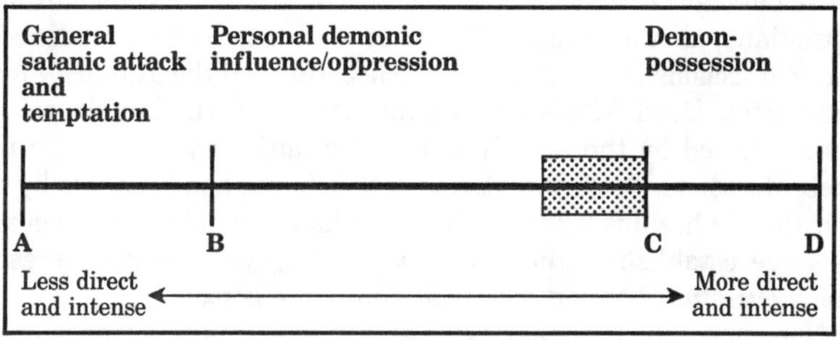

The line represents the entire spectrum of demonic activity toward people. The intensity of this activity increases from left to right on the line. The first section, between lines A and B, covers the general attacks of Satan toward all people, including believers. This includes temptation, opposition, and attempts to control. The second section, between lines B and C, covers all areas of demonic *oppression*. This may include influence through false teaching and even occultic activity. The third section, between lines C and D, covers demon *possession*, the internal dwelling by a demon or demons. The Bible itself does not give us a full description of everything demons are capable of. Because of this lack of accurate information, plus the satanic ability to deceive, plus our own shortcomings in the area of discernment, it is likely that certain activities, such as vocal chord control or even a demon throwing someone on the ground, may be caused by a demon without requiring internal habitation. This is indicated by the shaded area. To say anything more definite on this goes beyond the information that Scripture has given and is pure speculation on our part.

In the final analysis it is not necessary for us to define these differences, since God has not called us to be spiritual diagnosticians. No matter what the degree of demonic influence, the solution is the same: Christians are to "submit therefore to God. Resist the devil and he will flee from you" (James 4:7). At no point in Scripture is the solution for the believer phrased in such deliverance terminology as "binding" or "rebuking" the demon.

The Apostles and the Demonic

On three occasions the apostles are said to have been involved in the casting out of demons (Acts 8:5-8; 16:16-18; 19:11,12). None of these passages involves a debate over whether those delivered were Christians; all would agree that they were not. The significance of these exorcisms is as signs that the apostles had the authority from their risen Head (Christ) to act and speak on His behalf, as was demonstrated by the fact that they had authority over Satan like their Master. Once the foundation of the church had been laid by the apostles (Ephesians 2:20) and the boundary and nature of the gospel message established, the norm for dealing with demon-possessed unbelievers has become *the preaching of the gospel*.

Upon belief in Christ as Savior, an unbeliever is delivered not only from his sin but from any demonic influence which might have inflicted him. So the proper biblical way to deliver an unbeliever from demons is to *preach the gospel to him*. It does not do the victim any good for us to cast out demons, if we could, only to have him remain in his unsaved condition. Christ told the Pharisees in Matthew 12 that when the demon comes back to his old house and finds it swept and clean, he will go and get seven other demons, so that the state of the person will be worse than at the first. Any believer can deliver another person from demons by leading him to Christ. The Scriptures do not require a second step of deliverance for a believer in order that he may be freed from the demonic; Christ sweeps the house clean at the moment of salvation.

Our True Focus

Since Christians cannot be demon-possessed, they do not need to be delivered from the demonic. Satan can influence us from *without*, but God the Holy Spirit protects His children from internal repossession after salvation. One of the tragedies of the contemporary deliverance ministries is that they are attempting something which is a complete waste of time—trying to deliver Christians from demons. As we have noted in previous chapters, true spiritual warfare is primarily focused on the world and the flesh and not on preoccupation with demons. The focus of the Christian should be on proper ethical conduct in accordance with God's Word, and not on a metaphysical battle with Satan and his demons.

Increasingly Christians today seem to be getting caught up in preoccupation with Satan and the demonic. This has caused them to forget that there is a three-front war going on—not just with the devil, which is very real, but also with the world and the flesh. Many Christians have become so obsessed with Satan that they are being overrun on the other two fronts—the world and the flesh. In fact, many of the false teachings today about Satan and the demonic are really products of this world-system. Also, some of the very people who are at the forefront of the deliverance ministries are being overwhelmed by the flesh in many areas of their life because they think they are possessed by the devil instead of their own lusts.

The call for today is to let the Bible tell us who our real enemy is, what our battle plan involves, and how to carry it out. As holy rebels we must be completely submissive to Jesus Christ and His Word. Satan wants you to get your eyes on him; God wants you to get your eyes on Him and His Word.

– 8 –

Resisting the Attacker

Submit therefore to God. Resist the devil and he will flee from you.

—James 4:7

The Bible clearly teaches that Satan and his demons can attack and oppress Christians. Satan goes about as a roaring lion seeking whom he can devour. He and his demonic forces are an ever-present enemy against Christians. In the last chapter we saw the many ways that Satan and the demons can influence and affect Christians. What then is our defense against these enemies?

One form of popular teaching today focuses on the solution of deliverance or exorcism. According to this view, deliverance is not only for Christians but also for non-Christians. Usually deliverance is presented in terms of exorcism, rebuking, or binding Satan. However, it is exceptionally strange that we do not find any instructions or commands in Scripture for rebuking or binding Satan, but instead find the important command to *resist* the devil. This is found in three very important and similar passages in the New Testament: Ephesians 6:10-18; 1 Peter 5:6-9; and James 4:7. These passages not only give us great hope and confidence in spiritual warfare, but also give us great assurance that we cannot be blindsided by Satan.

The Problem of Fear

Much popular teaching today is fostering an attitude of fear among Christians. Recently an example of this came across my desk. The writer of this story is a former missionary who is now involved in a deliverance ministry.[1] At one time he did not believe that Christians could be demon-possessed, but then he had an experience which he

1. The following story is a summary of this article and all quotes are taken from it. From Ed Murphy, "My Daughter Demonized," in *Equipping the Saints,* Vol. 4, Winter 1990, pp. 27-29.

says completely changed his worldview. As we saw in the previous chapter, such a change is very common. But rather than coming to this change because of intensive Bible study, people are changing their views because they have some sort of experience which does not quite fit their previous understanding of Scripture. While we do not believe that Christians can be demon-possessed, and so question this writer's interpretation of his experience, other factors in the story raise an even greater concern: that of fostering fear and anxiety among Christians rather than confidence and hope.

The episode this author relates occurred in the 1960's, when his daughter was a young teenager. While away from home he received a very upsetting phone call from his wife, who insisted that he return home immediately because their daughter was acting strangely, and the wife believed she was demon-possessed. At that time he rejected this explanation, not believing that Christians could be demon-possessed. Nevertheless he quickly returned home and discovered a very frightened and confused daughter.

He began by questioning her about her relationship with the Lord. Her response, as he relates it, indicates a young girl who seemed to be walking with the Lord. She said, "Dad, help me. I'm scared. I love Jesus and I want to do what's right. What's wrong with me?" As he prayed with his daughter he noticed a pentagram on a chain hanging around her neck. In response to his inquiries she said that it was a gift from a friend. When he asked what it symbolized she replied, "I don't know; I guess it's kind of a good luck charm. It's found on the dust-covers of some musical albums. A lot of kids wear them."

After discovering the significance of the pentagram as a symbol of the occult, he told his daughter that she needed to remove it and renounce the spirit forces associated with it. As she obeyed, he says that they were immediately involved with a face-to-face confrontation with evil spirits. He prayed and renounced the demons associated with it, and after a second episode later that night he relates that she was finally delivered.

While it is beyond our intent to explain exactly what was taking place in this young girl's life, the way the story is told leaves us with some very important questions. If in fact this is a correct interpretation of the event, then we should have a legitimate fear that we too might unknowingly pick up a demon and become demon-possessed. At first glance the father seems to present his daughter as a fairly mature Christian for her age and one that is walking with the Lord. In complete innocence she had been introduced to occultic symbols and practices by a friend and thereby picked up a demon. Anyone who hears of an experience like this would wonder if he might innocently pick up a demon by unknowingly having an occult object lying around the house. If he or she walked through or by a store that sells such objects, might he not "pick up" a demon? In the story the father does seem to give some indication that the girl knew more than he first realized. Not only did she have the one pentagram necklace, but she had an entire box of occultic trinkets and had been exposed to heavier rock music and Transcendental Meditation (TM).

Asking Questions

The thinking Christian should think of several questions at this point. Can a Christian unknowingly be exposed to occultic objects and thereby pick up a demon and become demon oppressed or possessed? Second, if the involvement is innocent and done out of ignorance, where is the protection of a loving and sovereign God? Third, if this sort of thing happens (demonic oppression but not possession), what is to be the believer's response? What is the Christian to do to ward off the attacks of Satan in this age?

First Peter 5:8 is a well-known passage describing the strategy of Satan during this age as a roaring lion: "Be of sober spirit, be on the alert. Your adversary, the devil, prowls about like a roaring lion, seeking someone to devour." God in His wisdom not only warns us about the attacks of Satan, but also gives us clear instruction on how to deal with these attacks. This is described in the next verse: "But resist him, firm in your faith, knowing that the same experiences of suffering are being accomplished by your brethren in the world."

Some may think that resistance includes exorcism, so before we can look at the meaning of resisting the devil, we must first take a look at exorcism.

Is Exorcism an Option?

With the popularity of the movie *The Exorcist* (as well as the emphasis by deliverance teachers) the answer that many people expect the Bible to give to the problem of demonic oppression or possession is *exorcism*. However, as we have seen, this is not what the Bible actually teaches. The only people the Bible ever says cast out demons by the power of God were the Lord Jesus Christ, the apostles, and Philip. However, the Bible also records that unbelieving Jewish exorcists attempted to cast out demons in Jesus' name (Acts 19:13) and that there would be many people at the final judgment who had cast out demons in Jesus' name and performed many miracles in His name, but Jesus would reject them by saying, "I never knew you; depart from Me, you who practice lawlessness" (Matthew 7:23). The apparent or real casting out of demons neither validates the experience nor indicates that its practitioner is a child of God. In a recent interview, Paul Hiebert, professor in the World Mission department at Fuller Seminary, told of exorcism episodes he had witnessed in India in which Hindu gurus performed exorcisms and people were apparently delivered from demons. This was clearly not done by the power of God.

A prevalent attitude that seems to be communicated by deliverance ministries is that anyone oppressed or possessed by a demon should be delivered. It may surprise some that this apparently was not a view held by the apostle Paul. In Acts 16 we are told that when Paul and Silas were in Philippi, a slave girl who had a spirit of divination (a demon who gave her fortune-telling ability) followed them around giving an accurate testimony of their message. Many would think that Paul would have dealt with this problem early on, but he didn't. Acts 16:18 tells us that "she continued doing this for many days." Finally Paul became "greatly annoyed" and commanded the spirit to depart from her. Notice that he did not command the spirit to depart so he could witness to the girl, nor did he command the spirit to depart so he could have a better reception to his message, nor did he command the spirit to depart out of compassion or care for the girl. Instead, he commanded the spirit to depart because he was annoyed (probably because he did not want the truth he proclaimed to be impugned by a testimony from an evil spirit).

Signs and Wonders

When we examine the New Testament we find that the casting out of demons was one of the many miracles that came under the classification of signs and wonders. Acts 5:12 says, "At the hands of the apostles many signs and wonders were taking place among the people." The passage goes on to describe in detail what these signs and wonders consisted of: healing the sick as well as those afflicted with unclean spirits. Signs and wonders were specifically designed to authenticate and validate the ministry of the apostles; they were unique to them and those closely associated with them. If more than apostles could perform these signs and wonders, then the apostle Paul could not have said: "The signs of a true apostle were performed among you with all perseverance, by signs and wonders and miracles" (2 Corinthians 12:12). It is clear from these passages that the only legitimate practice of casting out demons as a sign or wonder was apostolic.

In some churches today there are those who maintain that the apostolic office has continued. While it is beyond the scope of this book to go into a lengthy discussion of this matter, let us say that the Bible does not support this view. Apostles were men who had witnessed the Lord's life and resurrection and had been directly commissioned by him (Acts 1:21,22). This office was a foundational office and thus unique to the beginnings of the church (Ephesians 2:20). Those who maintain the continuation of the office do so without scriptural basis. Since this gift/office has ceased, signs and wonders have also ceased, and with them the gift of exorcism.

This does not mean that God no longer performs miracles or delivers people from demons. During the time of our Lord's ministry on the earth and the beginning years of the church, God delegated the ability to perform miracles to a chosen few. These men performed these miracles through the power of God at their own discretion. They determined when they would perform these miracles and who they would heal. God mediated the miracles through these individuals. Today God still performs miracles and frees people from demons, but He performs this action *directly* rather than indirectly through His people. (Of course He may do it in response to the prayer of one person for another, or in response to the prayer of an unsaved person who turns to Christ and seeks salvation.) The writer of Hebrews, which was written late in the apostolic period, recognized that even by the late apostolic period, signs and wonders were a thing of the past (Hebrews 2:3,4). It is clear that the biblical solution to demonic oppression or possession in this age is never expressed in terms of exorcism, but rather in terms of resisting the devil.

How to Resist the Devil

The only command given to believers for dealing with Satan is to *resist* the devil. It is significant that this command is given three times in the New Testament (1 Peter 5:9; James 4:7; Ephesians 6:13). The word translated "resist" means "to stand against" or "to oppose." It is a compound of the Greek preposition *anti*, meaning "against," and *histami,* which means "to stand." The word came to mean "to set oneself against, to oppose, to resist, to withstand."

Ephesians 6:10-18 is the well-known passage where the believer is instructed to put on the armor of God. The reason given is so that he will be able to resist or stand against the devil. Notice that when Paul tells us why we are to put on the armor he says that it will enable us to *stand against (anthistami)* (verse 13), but also that we may be able to *stand firm.* The word for "stand firm" is simply another form of the word used for "resist." It is the Greek word *histami,* which means "to stand." We resist the devil by putting on the armor of God.

This word group reflects a military usage. It is the word that was used in orders given to a sentry. His responsibility was primarily *defensive* rather than *offensive,* since a sentry's responsibility is to guard the encampment or fortress and to watch for the enemy. If the enemy is spotted or seeks to infiltrate the camp, then the guard is to alert the troops so they can defend their position. It is not the guard's responsibility to go on the offensive, to seek out and engage the enemy.

It is extremely important to pay attention to the *defensive* aspect of this command, since it is just the opposite of what some people are teaching today about spiritual warfare. The ideas of binding, rebuking, or taking dominion over Satan and demonic strongholds are *offensive* ideas. When believers go on the offensive against Satan they are stepping out of their legitimate bounds by becoming involved in situations which the Lord has never intended for them. This offensive type of response was described by Peter as characteristic of false teachers (2 Peter 2:10,11). Often this opens the door to demonic oppression in the believer's life.

Just as a guard who spotted the enemy and went out to engage him would be dangerously exposed to the attacks of the enemy, so a believer is vulnerable to increased satanic attack when he stops resisting and starts attacking. Perhaps some churches have so many people who have problems with demons is because they are involved in an aggressive campaign against Satan which has put them in a position of biblical disobedience and opened them up to demonic oppression. We must recognize that the battle is the Lord's and not ours. No amount of spiritualizing with religious terminology can transform binding and rebuking into some form of defensive language.

Standing Firm

A beautiful example of what is meant by standing firm is found in the flight of Israel from Egypt. As the Israelites followed the Lord's command to leave Egypt they were followed by Pharaoh and all his chariots and calvary and infantry. Pharaoh represented the greatest military establishment at that time, and he threw everything he had against the Israelites. This threat surely overwhelmed them and struck fear in their hearts—a situation not very different from the Christian who is the target of Satan. When the Israelites in their fear accused Moses of bringing them out of Egypt to be killed, Moses demonstrated the kind of attitude and action which Christians are to have in spiritual warfare: "Do not fear! Stand by and see the salvation of the Lord.... The Lord will fight for you while you keep silent" (Exodus 14:13,14). As they obeyed and stood firm, the Lord delivered them first by opening up the Red Sea as a path of escape and then by drowning the army of Pharaoh in the waters as they closed back on them.

The Israelites were to stand firm; this was their responsibility. The Lord would deliver; that was His responsibility. In the same way believers today are to stand firm against Satan; that is our responsibility. We are to stand our ground in our position in Christ. God then deals with Satan. We are on the defensive, and God exercises the option of the offensive.

How to Put on the Armor of God

When we ask specifically how we are to resist or stand firm against the devil, the Scriptures are clear: Christians are to resist or stand against the devil by putting on the full armor of God. Twice Paul states this in Ephesians 6 to make sure we get the point. Just as a guard would put on his armor and collect his weapons before going out to his watch post, so the believer is to put on his armor so that he will be able to stand firm.

This passage on spiritual warfare begins by instructing the Christian to "be strong in the Lord and in the strength of His might" (Ephesians 6:10). This reminds us not only of Moses' statement to the Israelites that they were to stand still and see the deliverance of the Lord, but also of David's statement that the battle is the Lord's.

In the Old Testament one of the titles given to God is that of Lord of Hosts, or Lord of the Armies. This refers to His position as Commander-in-Chief over all the angelic hosts. Once we become citizens of heaven we are to submit ourselves to His authority as the Commanding General. It is in *His* strength that we fight, and according to *His* orders.

This means first and foremost that we must submit ourselves to Him and His lordship if we are to have victory in our holy rebellion. Submission involves the attitude of humility. This is why the two other passages related to standing against the devil emphasize the attitude of humility. Peter tells us, "Clothe yourselves with humility toward one another, for God is opposed to the proud, but gives grace to the humble. Humble yourselves therefore under the mighty hand of God, that He may exalt you at the proper time" (1 Peter 5:5,6). James' command is almost identical in 4:6 and 4:10. It is between these two sentences that he says, "Submit therefore to God. Resist the devil and he will flee from you."

This is a great promise from God. When we submit ourselves to God as our Lord and as the Commander-in-Chief of the warfare, then we are exhibiting humility. It is no longer *our* will but *His* which we follow. This attitude of humility was exemplified by Jesus Christ when He clothed Himself with humanity, by taking the position and form of a bondservant and humbling Himself by becoming obedient to the point of death (Philippians 2:8,9).

The essence of humility is to put ourselves in the position of a servant of God and to give up all claim to personal rights. Jesus expressed this principle when He said, "If anyone wishes to come after Me, let him deny himself, and take up his cross, and follow Me" (Matthew 16:24). If we are going to take up the full armor of God and operate in His strength, we must first humble ourselves under the mighty hand of God.

It is only with such an attitude of humility that we are able to submit ourselves to God and put on the full armor. But before we look at the armor there are some things we must understand. First, the armor passage is simply an analogy. We must be careful not to read too much into each piece. The armor is simply a visual aid to help us understand what it means to put on Jesus Christ (Romans 13:14). "Putting on Christ" means to put on the *character* of Christ. In essence putting on the armor is an illustration of the Christian life: By putting on His character we will be able to stand firm against the schemes of the devil, just as Jesus did when He was tested in the wilderness.

Six Pieces of Armor

There are two aspects to putting on the full armor of God. The first looks at putting on the full armor, while the second looks at each individual piece. When we decide to follow the Lord Jesus in spiritual warfare and submit to Him, in one sense we put on the full armor. This doesn't necessarily mean that every piece is fully in place, needing no more adjustment, but the armor as a whole is in place. When we first trust Christ as our Savior we become identified with Him and receive His righteousness. This is called *positional sanctification* or *positional holiness*. Because our position is "in Christ" we are credited and clothed in the eyes of God with His perfect righteousness.

Yet even though we are positionally righteous and holy, we still sin and we still need to grow as Christians. This is known as *progressive sanctification*. It is the progressive, step-by-step, day-by-day walk of the believer in which he gradually does away with the sin in his life and begins to live in obedience to God. To summarize, *positional sanctification* is putting on the full armor of God, while *progressive sanctification* focuses on each piece.

In the Book of Joshua the Israelites invaded the land of Canaan to take it for themselves, as God commanded. When they first entered the land they had a few pitched battles and conquered some key towns, such as Jericho and Ai. After these victories they were basically in control of the land, but the battle was not over. They were in control *positionally*, but not *totally*, since they still had to carry on a mopping-up operation. This involved years of taking out different pockets of resistance.

The armor that Paul described in Ephesians 6 contains six pieces. Many interpreters believe that the idea of this illustration came to Paul as he was in Rome under house arrest, probably chained to one or two guards. As he observed their armor and readiness for battle he drew on this phenomenon to illustrate how the believer is to defend himself against the schemes of the devil. Paul clearly used this illustration to make a particular point, since he did not mention every piece of armor that a Roman soldier might wear. It is important to note the order in which he presented these pieces.

The belt of truth. The first thing we need to do to be successful in spiritual warfare is to *put on the belt of truth*. For a Roman soldier the belt was a very important piece of equipment. A Roman soldier normally wore a long, free-flowing tunic. This would obviously get in his way if he were in a battle, hindering his movements. So he would strap a belt around his waist, then pull the loose ends of the tunic through it in order to keep it out of his way. This prepared him for action and kept him from stumbling or being hindered by the tunic.

Jesus used this same phrase in Luke 12:35: "Be dressed in readiness." The idea of putting on the belt emphasizes *readiness, preparation, watchfulness*, and *alertness*. This same idea of removing hindrances is found in Hebrews 12:1. There the analogy is a race, and we are to "lay aside every encumbrance, and the sin which so easily entangles us." Using the soldier illustration in his second letter to Timothy, Paul reminded him that a good soldier wouldn't get tangled up with the affairs of this life, or else it would hinder his success as a good fighter (2 Timothy 2:4).

The belt that removes the hindrances to our fight and prepares us for the battle is the belt of *truth*. Truth in this verse refers to *the Word of God as objective truth*. Some have suggested that this refers to truthfulness or integrity, since the sword mentioned later is also the Word of God. But there the idea is the Word of God put to use in *specific situations*. The belt of truth cannot refer to general truthfulness and personal integrity, since these are inadequate as a preparation for warfare against satanic forces. It is only *the Word of God* which prepares us and instructs us about sin in our lives, so that we may remove the sin which hinders us in our spiritual warfare.

Jesus stressed the necessity of the Scriptures for sanctification when He said, "You shall know the truth, and the truth shall make you free" (John 8:32). It is only when we personally put on the belt of truth, committing ourselves to the absolute truth and sufficiency of God's Word, that we are freed from hindrances in spiritual warfare. The reason many Christians today are ineffective in their Christian life and in spiritual warfare is because they have not committed themselves fully to the Word of God, which alone is sufficient to prepare them for every situation in life. Often the Christian today falls into the trap we explained in Chapter 2: that of merging the Bible with other forms of truth. Rather than taking the Bible alone, many people today are merging the divine viewpoint of the Bible with the human viewpoint of psychology or sociology or self-help techniques. They are trying to solve the problems in their lives not by Christ alone, but by Christ plus something else. This has left them dangerously handicapped in carrying out their rebellion against Satan. In fact, by taking the Bible plus something else they are doing exactly what Satan wants them to do.

The breastplate of righteousness. No Roman soldier would ever go into a battle without his breastplate on. At times Roman soldiers used breastplates made of leather or animal hooves, although the most common breastplate was a solid piece of metal which covered the front of the soldier's torso from the base of the neck to the upper thighs. This protected all his vital organs, including the heart and the bowels.

In the Bible the heart and the bowels are very significant because they were used to represent the immaterial part of man. The heart was often used to refer to the mind and at times to the emotions, although the bowels were more often used to represent the emotions. Proverbs 3:5 instructs us, "Trust in the Lord with all your heart, and do not lean on your own understanding." Proverbs 4:23 warns us, "Watch over your heart with all diligence, for from it flow the springs of life."

In the original languages of the Scriptures the bowels or kidneys are used to represent emotions. Many times when we are in a very emotional condition, such as worry or anger, we feel it in our stomach. The King James Version translates Philippians 2:1 literally, "... if any bowels and mercies." Often the word translated "compassion" in English has the sense of "bowels" in the original Greek.

The point of all this is that our thoughts and emotions are to be protected from Satan's attacks by the *breastplate of righteousness.* Some of Satan's primary tactics are to influence people through false doctrine and through reliance upon their emotions rather than on the truth of God's Word. In order to protect the mind and emotions, the Christian is to put on the breastplate of righteousness.

This righteousness has two aspects. The first is the *righteousness of Christ* which has been imputed or credited to us: "To the one who does not work, but believes in Him who justifies the ungodly, his faith is reckoned as righteousness" (Romans 4:5). Righteousness refers to our right standing before God. Satan and his demons often attack the Christian by raising doubts about his salvation or his relationship with God, or by accusing the believer because of sin in his life. The only basis we have for response to such attacks is that our standing before God has nothing to do with our own righteousness, but is solely and completely based on the righteousness of Jesus Christ. However, there is more to putting on the breastplate of righteousness then just enjoying our positional righteousness in Christ.

The second aspect involves our *personal righteousness*. This does not refer to our own goodness, for we have none. Instead, it refers to the righteousness and holiness produced in our lives by the Holy Spirit as a result of our growth in Christ and obedience to God. This is the progressive part of our sanctification.

Although every believer is positionally righteous in Christ, he is also responsible to pursue holiness in his life by being obedient to Christ and having his character transformed and conformed to the character of Christ. This takes place in a believer's life as he recognizes the sin in his life and then turns away from it and turns to Christ. Peter also relates this to dealing with the lusts of the flesh: "As obedient children, do not be conformed to the former lusts which were yours in your ignorance, but like the Holy One who called you, be holy yourselves also in all your behavior; because it is written, 'You shall be holy, for I am holy'" (1 Peter 1:14-16).

This is part of what is meant by standing firm against the devil. In James 4:7-10 we see that this concept is related not only to the idea of submission and humility but also to cleansing ourselves from sin. James 4:8 says, "Draw near to God and He will draw near to you. Cleanse your hands, you sinners, and purify your hearts, you double-minded." While the believer is continually cleansed by the blood of Christ for all sins, he realizes this cleansing in his life in a practical way by confessing his sins: "If we confess our sins, He is faithful and righteous to forgive us our sins and to cleanse us from all unrighteousness" (1 John 1:9).

Whenever a Christian sins, in essence he is giving his loyalty to Satan and rebelling like a child against his Father. At this point the Christian is being influenced by either his flesh or the world to follow Satan in obedience. At the point of sin the Christian opens himself up to Satanic attack. Once this breach in his defense occurs, if he does not turn from his sin but continues in it, that toehold which Satan has in his life may be expanded. Eventually the believer can be living in full-blown rebellion against God. At some point it is possible that the believer can become involved with some aspect of the occult and become oppressed by a demon. This is exactly what happened in the life of King Saul in the Old Testament, and it eventually resulted in demonic oppression, severe depression, and involvement in the occult.

However, as with Saul, the solution to the problem of demonic oppression and sin is simply to turn from sin. Many times God gave Saul the opportunity to turn from his sin, but because he never did, God continued to discipline him through the demonic oppression.

This same thing occurred in the New Testament. In two different instances the New Testament tells about Christians who had fallen into serious and prolonged sin, and because they failed to turn from it they were given over to Satan for discipline (1 Corinthians 5:5; 1 Timothy 1:20). The solution to this problem is never presented in the Scriptures in any way except turning from sin and turning to God. If the believer does this, Satan will flee.

Feet shod with the preparation of the gospel of peace. Today shoes are often purchased on the basis of fashion and not function. But anyone who works on his or her feet (or jogs or hikes) knows the value of a well-made pair of shoes or boots. Roman soldiers also valued their shoes because they realized that their effectiveness in combat could well depend on the sureness of their footing. They wore sandals, heavy soles bound to their feet with leather straps. The bottoms of the soles were reinforced with hobnails or studs to give added protection against spikes or stakes stuck in the ground for defense.

The spiritual shoes worn by Christians likewise give them a sure-footed stance against the devil, as well as protection. The shoes are described as "the preparation" of the gospel of peace. Literally that means *readiness*. What prepares or makes us ready, what gives us stability and protection against the attacks of Satan, is the "gospel of peace."

Scripture tells us that before we were saved we were enemies of God, but that the death of Christ is the basis for our reconciliation: "If while we were enemies we were reconciled to God through the death of His Son, much more, having been reconciled, we shall be saved by His life" (Romans 5:10). When we trust Christ as our Savior we are justified by faith. The result of this is that we now have peace with God: "Therefore having been justified by faith, we have peace with God through our Lord Jesus Christ" (Romans 5:1). This is the gospel of peace—the fact that we are at peace with God, that we have been transferred permanently to the kingdom of His Son, and that we are now on His side against the rebellion of Satan. This is our new position in Christ, and it is on the basis of this new position that we are able to resist the devil.

This means that whenever we find ourselves tempted to doubt or to sin, because of our position in Christ as a child of God (and because we are at peace with God) we can stand firm. Satan can attack and tempt all he wants, but it need never phase us. We can remain steadfast and immovable because our feet are firmly grounded on our immovable relationship with God.

The shield of faith. Although Roman soldiers carried one of two types of shields, it is the larger one that is mentioned here. This shield was a very large oblong shield, some four feet tall and 2½ feet wide. It was used by the soldier to hide behind in protection from the arrows and flaming missiles which the enemy would hurl at him.

The shield that protects the Christian is the shield of *faith.* Faith means to trust God. No matter what the situation and no matter how difficult God's instructions might seem, we are to trust in God. "Without faith it is impossible to please Him, for he who comes to God must believe that He is, and that He is a rewarder of those who seek Him" (Hebrews 11:6). It is only by *believing God* that we can avoid the traps and snares that Satan sets for us. Adam and Eve fell into Satan's trap in the Garden of Eden because they trusted in their own ability rather than in God's Word. This is Satan's major weapon—to get us to distrust God's Word. Whenever we sin we are believing Satan and giving our allegiance to him.

With the shield of faith we are not only able to extinguish in a general sense the missiles Satan throws at the world, but we are able to extinguish *all* the missiles Satan throws at us. By trusting God and obeying Him we need not worry about any attack that Satan might use; every trick he tries can be handled by simply trusting God.

The helmet of salvation. The Roman soldier's helmet was made of leather and metal and was designed to protect his head against arrows and swords. What protects the Christian is his *salvation.* However, Paul is not saying that the person needs *to get* saved, since he already is or else he wouldn't be wearing the other pieces of the armor.

In earlier chapters we mentioned the three phases of our salvation which the New Testament describes. The first phase is called *justification.* This takes place when a person puts his trust in Christ for his salvation. This is salvation from the penalty of sin. The second phase is *sanctification.* This is the phase known as the Christian life, when we learn God's Word and apply it in order to be delivered from the power of sin. The third phase is *glorification*, when a Christian goes to heaven and is freed from the very presence of sin.

The helmet of salvation speaks of the application of God's Word to our present life on earth. This is phase two of our salvation. Paul speaks of this in Philippians 2:12, where we are instructed to work out our salvation with fear and trembling. We put on the helmet of salvation by letting the principles of God's Word renew and transform our minds.

The sword of the Spirit, which is the Word of God. The sword mentioned here is the short sword which the Roman soldier carried. It was used in close combat and was a weapon that had to be used in a very precise manner. Its function was primarily defensive, since it was used to ward off the close-range attacks of the enemy. It was not the large broadsword, which would be the weapon of choice in an offensive campaign.

The sword which the Christian carries is described here as the Word of God. But this is not the Word of God generally. The term translated "word" here is not the Greek *logos*, but *rhema. Rhema* refers to a *specific* word or utterance. In spiritual warfare it is not enough to have merely a *general* knowledge of the Scriptures; we must also have a *specific* knowledge of the Scriptures and use this knowledge correctly.

This was graphically demonstrated by our Lord when He faced His temptation in the wilderness. When Satan tested the Lord, Jesus did not attack or rebuke Satan, but countered his thrusts with specific parries from Scripture. When Satan tempted the Lord he displayed a knowledge of Scripture, but he twisted it and used it in inappropriate ways. Because Jesus had an excellent and accurate knowledge of the Scripture He was able to defend Himself against Satan. In the same way the Christian is able to defend himself against the attacks of Satan by using Scripture accurately. This means that we must know Scripture well enough to use it in any situation, and to use it correctly. One reason many Christians are ineffective in the battle against Satan is that they have only a partial (and in many cases inaccurate) knowledge of Scripture.

God's Promise to You

We are to take up a defensive posture against Satan and submit ourselves to God. As we resist the devil with an attitude of humility and submission to God, we are promised that God will take care of the battle for us, and Satan will flee. The picture here is of two different forces. On the one hand is the believer, whose responsibility is the defensive, while on the other is the Lord and the holy angels, whose responsibility is the offensive. When we rest in our proper position, the Lord and His angels attack from the flank and defeat Satan.

Perhaps you have been plagued by demonic manifestations. Perhaps you were involved in the occult before you were saved, or have become involved since then. But whatever the reason, perhaps you are facing serious spiritual oppression. If so, the significance of Ephesians 6 must not be lost on you, since it is a passage of great comfort. When you are under attack by Satan you need to rest in your position in Christ, trust in His Word, and submit to God. The result will be that Satan and his hosts must flee. This is God's promise to you.

– 9 –

The Greatest Weapon

Confess your sins to one another, and pray for one another, so that you may be healed. The effective prayer of a righteous man can accomplish much.

—James 5:16

In the last chapter we saw that the Bible gives us clear instructions on how to have victory in our struggle with the forces of Satan: We are to simply put on the whole armor of God and thereby resist the devil. But even though this is simple in concept, it is not so easy to do in actual daily living. As Paul concludes his description of the armor, he makes a very important statement which we all too often overlook in our practical daily experience:

> With all prayer and petition pray at all times in the Spirit, and with this in view be on the alert with all perseverance and petition for all the saints (Ephesians 6:18).

The action which undergirds and strengthens the armor is twofold: *prayer* and *perseverance*. These are vitally important for today, yet so lacking in the lives of many Christians that we want to take two chapters to focus on what these two things mean and how they apply in daily spiritual warfare.

Does Prayer Really Change Things?

Prayer is so often mentioned and commanded in Scripture that its necessity can hardly be questioned. But why should we pray? After all, if God is sovereign and works all things after the counsel of His will (Ephesians 1:11), why bother asking God to do something, since He has already determined what He will do? Another way this question is sometimes phrased is this: Does prayer really change things?

Prayer is simply communication to God by a Christian. Prayer as seen in Scripture may contain one or more of the following elements: confession, adoration, praise, thanksgiving, intercession for others, and petition for oneself. Prayer is the means by which a believer's communion with God is strengthened. In prayer we pour out our souls to God, and in the process our souls are nourished, our spirits are revitalized, our attitudes are conformed to God's character, and our focus is sharpened by the promises of God. In short, our ability to stand firm is strengthened.

In spiritual warfare three aspects of prayer are important. The first aspect is *thanksgiving*. Often in the heat of the battle when we are faced with discouragements or suffering there is a strong temptation to become self-oriented and cave in to self-pity and the "poor me" syndrome. We begin to focus on the problem and the conflict and forget that the Lord is battling for us. As time goes on, spiritual fatigue sets in. This is why prayer and perseverance are so often linked together. In prayer we are rested, refreshed, and refocused on the work of God in our lives.

The second aspect of prayer that is vital in spiritual warfare is *confession*. Confession means that we recognize sin in our lives and admit it to God. The attitude underlying confession is humility. We recognize that we have failed God and have been disobedient. Underlying confession is the realization of our own dependence upon God and our inability to fully meet His standards. First John 1:9 promises that "if we confess our sins He is faithful and righteous to forgive us our sins and to cleanse us from all unrighteousness." The word translated "cleanse" here is the same word used in James 4:8: "Cleanse your hands, you sinners." As we saw in the previous chapter, the entire statement of James 4:6-10 must be taken together. That passage is framed by statements in verses 6 and 10 to be humble, because true humility involves confession of sin. This is part of what we must do in submitting to God and resisting the devil. This is what it means to draw near to God. As we do this we are promised that God will draw near to us.

The third aspect of prayer that is vital in spiritual warfare is *petition*. As we encounter opposition and hostility in the world from the flesh, the world, or Satan, we call upon God to come to our aid. This again demonstrates the basic attitude which is foundational to spiritual warfare, namely *humility*. In prayer we adopt an attitude of submission and humility toward God. We call on Him to intercede in our behalf.

Total Dependence

The primary image of prayer in the Bible is that of a subordinate coming to his superior to make requests. It emphasizes the attitude of total dependence even when the request is known beforehand to be the will and the desire of the superior. Even though an employee (let's say a sales manager) may know that his boss wants him to conduct regular training sessions with the sales force, he still needs to go to his boss to arrange times, coordinate the meetings with other events, and confirm permission for what he is doing. This demonstrates his submission to his boss and his recognition that he serves a higher authority.

In prayer we go to God in dependence, asking for what we already know is generally the will of God, requesting God's aid in certain areas, and then waiting on the Lord to work out the details. Sometimes our request may be generally within the will of God but in this specific instance outside God's sovereign will. It may be a matter of timing (when God is simply saying wait), or it may be a matter of God simply denying the request. Sometimes God's denials are hard for us to comprehend, especially when these involve prolonged suffering, poverty, unemployment, sickness, or living in a difficult relationship. At those times we are tempted to impatiently attempt to solve the problem on our own terms rather than wait on the Lord. We need to *persevere in our dependence.*

Sometimes we wonder why God doesn't answer certain of our prayers, especially when it seems to us that they are completely within God's will. After all, we have the promise in 1 John 5:14,15: "This is the confidence which we have before Him, that if we ask anything according to His will, He hears us. And if we know that He hears us in whatever we ask, we know that we have the requests which we have asked from Him." This passage clearly states that when we ask according to God's will, He will answer. Other prayer promises that Jesus made also indicate that when we come to the Father in Jesus' name, He will hear and answer us.

> Whatever you ask in My name, that will I do, that the Father may be glorified in the Son. If you ask Me anything in My name, I will do it (John 14:13,14).
>
> If you abide in Me, and My words abide in you, ask whatever you wish, and it shall be done for you (John 15:7).

> All things you ask in prayer, believing, you shall receive (Matthew 21:22).

Must God Answer Prayer?

These great promises of Scripture which indicate God's certain answers to our prayers raise another question: If we follow all the guidelines presented in the Bible for prayer, does this obligate God to answer our prayers? The answer to this is both yes and no. It is *yes* in the sense that when we pray according to God's clear promises to us, God is obligated to answer (exactly what we mean by this will be clarified later in the chapter), although the timing is up to Him. But the answer is also *no*, for three reasons. First, we often link the "when" and the "how" to the general prayer request. This puts man the creature in control of God the Creator. In current spiritual-warfare practice, the prayers of many people, while expressed in words that indicate a request, are in fact nothing more than commands by the believer toward God to intercede in a particular way. This is pride, not humility. A proud approach in prayer makes this type of prayer satanic rather than holy. Whenever we do anything in pride we are following Satan in his rebellion.

Petition is essentially the request of a child to a father to intercede and protect. How this is done and when it is done are left completely to the sovereign will of the Father.

A very important prayer promise is found in James 5:16b: "The effective prayer of a righteous man can accomplish much." James then draws upon the prayers of Elijah to illustrate this principle. But before we look at Elijah to find several principles characteristic of efficacious praying, we must first ask what "efficacious praying" is.

The King James Version translates this phrase "the effective fervent prayer." This is similar to the New American Standard translation and seems to imply the idea that fervency somehow makes prayer more effective. Some take this to mean that the harder we pray the more effective the prayer, thereby treating prayer as something mystical or magical. Some churches have been known to promote marathon prayer sessions based on this interpretation. However, the Bible always distinguishes between prayer and magic.

The difficulty with this verse is the unusual Greek construction. Without laboring the point, we suggest that the most consistent way to understand this verse is by realizing that it is not the *prayer itself* that is strong or efficacious but *the One who answers*. The best way to understand this is probably to understand it as "the prayer of a righteous man accomplishes much when it is effective."[1] Elijah furnishes the example of how much can be accomplished through prayer.

Elijah and the Promise

Effective prayer is based on the promises of God. The specific instance mentioned by James occurred at the beginning of Elijah's ministry. James 5:17,18 states: "He prayed earnestly that it might not rain; and it did not rain on the earth for three years and six months. And he prayed again, and the sky poured rain, and the earth produced its fruit." The incident is recorded in 1 Kings 17:1–18:45.

Elijah's ministry was to the northern kingdom of Israel during the time of the divided kingdom. Ahab the king of Israel had married Jezebel, the daughter of the high priest of Baal worship in Tyre, who used her position as queen to impose and advance the worship of Baal in the northern kingdom. She instigated a policy of executing any known prophet of God. (This was one of the darkest periods in the history of Israel.) The few prophets who remained alive were hiding in caves, and the people gave themselves completely to the idolatrous worship of Baal and the Asherah.

It was at this time that Elijah suddenly and abruptly appeared on the scene announcing God's judgment on Israel for their rebellion. The judgment announced is grounded in the promise of God in the Mosaic law. As Israel prepared to enter the land that God had promised to give them, Moses reminded the people of their covenant obligations to obey God. Part of the covenant contained promises of blessing for obedience and warnings of judgment for disobedience. There was a specific judgement mentioned for idolatry: "Beware lest your hearts be deceived and you turn away and serve other gods and worship them. Or the anger of the Lord will be kindled against you, and He will shut up the heavens so that there will be no rain and the ground will not yield its fruit; and you will perish quickly from the good land which the Lord is giving you" (Deuteronomy 11:16,17).

Elijah was able to stand before the powerful king of Israel and announce this judgment on him because he knew the promise of God. We are not told whether God specifically told Elijah to confront Ahab

---

1. James 5:16, Peter David's Commentary on James, New International Greek Testament Commentary (Grand Rapids, MI, Eerdmans, 1983), pp. 196-97.

or whether Elijah simply knew the promises of God and applied them to his situation. (We believe that the latter is more likely, especially since 1 Kings 18:1 specifically states that God told Elijah to go to Ahab to announce the end of the drought.) But in either case Elijah's actions were grounded on the promise of God.

Between the time that God instructed Elijah to announce to Ahab the termination of the drought and the coming of rain two things happened: Elijah confronted the prophets of Baal demonstrating the impotence of their god, and he prayed to the Lord. It is this prayer which yields principles of effective praying. First and foremost it was a prayer based on the promises of God. As Peter tells us:

> His divine power has granted to us everything pertaining to life and godliness, through the true knowledge of Him who called us by His own glory and excellence. For by these He has granted to us His precious and magnificent promises, in order that by them you might become partakers of the divine nature, having escaped the corruption that is in the world by lust (2 Peter 1:3,4 NASB).

Is Every Promise Made to Me?

At this point we must warn against wrongly applying God's promises. Someone has stated that there are over 7000 promises in the Bible, but not all of those promises are for Christians. It is important to distinguish between promises given to specific individuals, to the nation Israel, to the disciples, and to the church.

Some promises are individual in nature. For example, God made specific promises to David, Moses, Elijah, Mary, and the disciples. These promises were conditioned by certain historical events and are not to be applied to anyone else, as we will see. One example of an individual promise that is often used in contemporary spiritual-warfare contexts to justify the practice of casting out demons is Jesus' statement to His disciples in Matthew 10:7,8: "As you go, preach, saying, 'the kingdom of heaven is at hand.' Heal the sick, raise the dead, cleanse the lepers, cast out demons; freely you received, freely give."

Based on just these two verses it would seem justifiable to suggest, as some do today, that these four activities should accompany the proclamation of the gospel. This view has come to be known as "power evangelism." Casting out demons, it is suggested, should be one of the things accompanying the true preaching of the gospel. But before we decide whether this is true, we must consider the entire statement that Jesus made. These two verses must not be removed or isolated from the entire commission that Jesus gave His disciples at that time. For example, not only did He command them to heal the sick and cast out demons but He also prohibited them from going to the Gentiles, limiting them to the house of Israel only (Matthew 10:5,6). Immediately after His instructions regarding the message they were to proclaim, Jesus also prohibited His disciples from accepting any money or taking any supplies or luggage with them—even an extra change of clothes or shoes. We suggest that if this promise of Jesus to cast out demons is valid for today, than these other conditions must also be met. This is the kind of problem that results from misapplying Scripture and taking verses out of context.

Other Promises

Another type of promise is that given to the nation of Israel. The Old Testament is filled with promises meant only for Israel and related explicitly to their obedience to the Mosaic law. Yet often these verses are taken out of context, and God is expected to fulfill promises to the church or the United States which were meant only for Israel. One example of this error is the use of 2 Chronicles 7:14: "If... My people who are called by My name humble themselves and pray, and seek My face and turn from their wicked ways, then I will hear from heaven, will forgive their sin, and will heal their land." Even a superficial look at the surrounding verses shows that this was a statement made to Solomon concerning God's people Israel at the dedication of the temple. The phrase "heal their land" is a reference to the judgment of drought mentioned in the previous verse, which itself is a restatement to Solomon of the passage quoted earlier (Deuteronomy 11:16,17). In 2 Chronicles 7 God is reaffirming His covenant promises to Israel with Solomon. Since the Mosaic covenant was made with Israel, the promise of verse 14 must be understood in that context and applied only to Israel.

Still another type of promise is general or universal. While many promises in the Old Testament are specifically addressed to certain individuals or to Israel, many others are general. We are certainly not trying to imply that the Old Testament has no relevance for Christians today; we simply want to caution you to make sure that when you hold God to a promise, that promise was not intended for someone else.

Now here are some general New Testament promises to Christians.

> I can do all things through Him who strengthens me (Philippians 4:13).
>
> God has not destined us for wrath, but for obtaining salvation through our Lord Jesus Christ (1 Thessalonians 5:9).
>
> We know that God causes all things to work together for good to those who love God, to those who are called according to His purpose (Romans 8:28,29).
>
> I am convinced that neither death, nor life, nor angels, nor principalities, nor things present, nor things to come, nor powers, nor height, nor depth, nor any other created thing, shall be able to separate us from the love of God, which is in Christ Jesus our Lord (Romans 8:38,39).

Using God's Promises Correctly

All promises, even general ones, ought to be used correctly. One often-misused promise is found in Matthew 18:19, immediately following Jesus' statement that "whatever you shall bind on earth shall be bound in heaven, and whatever you loose on earth shall be loosed in heaven" (verse 18). In Chapter 6 we discussed the meaning of this passage. The context is one of church discipline and the language is courtroom language. This is also true for Matthew 18:19: "Again I say to you that if two of you agree on earth about anything that they may ask, it shall be done for them by My Father who is in heaven."

Often this passage is applied to any type of prayer: Whenever any two Christians agree together in prayer, then God is obligated to answer that prayer. But the context shows that this is a promise related to the execution of *church discipline*, or excommunication. The "two" mentioned in verse 19 and the "two or three" mentioned in verse 20 are the same two or three witnesses that testify against the accused in verse 16. Christians need to be careful that they are not led astray into wrong prayer methods by incorrectly applying this verse.

Elijah could have the boldness to confront Ahab and announce the drought because he correctly understood and applied the promise of God in Deuteronomy 11. Since this was a national promise of divine discipline on Israel for idolatry, Elijah could confidently expect God to fulfill His promise. After three years of drought God directed Elijah to go to Ahab and announce the return of rain. This was an individual promise to Elijah, so Elijah could confidently expect God to bring rain to the land.

Since God made this specific promise to Elijah, why did Elijah still pray for rain? In 1 Kings 18:41,42 Elijah announced the coming rain to Ahab and immediately went to the top of Mount Carmel and began to pray. Often we make the mistake of generally trusting God without backing it up with prayer, but Elijah continued to humble himself in prayer even though God had specifically promised the rain. Often our general reliance upon God without specific prayer reveals a subtle influence of pride. But Elijah shows us that even though we have a specific promise from God, we must continue to pray to God. Perseverance in prayer is critical.

Get Alone with God

Too often in our busy lives, pressed as we are by the demands of people and the overcrowding of our calendars, the one thing that gets lost is our personal time alone with God. Yet the prayer lives of the great saints of Scripture reveals how often they took time to get alone with God. After announcing the coming rain to Ahab, Elijah withdrew from the crowds to pray. He recognized that crushing crowds and crunching calendars may destroy communion and fellowship with God. We simply *must* withdraw and get alone with God.

When our Lord was on the earth He recognized the same truth. Several times the Bible mentions that after busy times of ministry, when the press of the crowds and the demands of ministry closed in around Him, Jesus withdrew to be alone with God. One busy day began with the news that John the Baptist had been executed, and in response Jesus withdrew to be alone (Matthew 14:13). But His disciples found Him and the crowds followed Him, and He spent the rest of the day healing the sick. When evening came He miraculously multiplied five loaves of bread and two fish to feed them all. After a busy day like this many of us would crash on the couch in front of the TV or head off to bed early, but not our Lord. He realized that He was in need of spiritual revitalization, so "after He had sent the multitudes away, He went up to the mountain by Himself to pray; and when it was evening, He was there alone" (Matthew 14:23). Jesus recognized the importance of time in communion with the Father. If He who was one with the Father needed to spend time in prayer alone with the

Father, how much more do we who are His children, yet still sinners, need to be alone pouring out our hearts to the Father.

As reports of Jesus' teaching and healing ministry traveled throughout the land, people poured out of the villages to hear Him and to be healed. We can only imagine the demands this put on Jesus' time, yet in spite of this He never failed to get alone with God and pray: "The news about Him was spreading even farther, and great multitudes were gathering to hear Him and to be healed of their sicknesses. But He Himself would often slip away to the wilderness and pray" (Luke 5:15,16).

Another important time for prayer is during times of decision-making. Jesus exemplified this before He chose His disciples. We are not told what He prayed for, but simply that He prayed. And He didn't pray for just 15 or 20 minutes, but "He spent the whole night in prayer to God" (Luke 6:12).

We must ask ourselves at this point how often we spend even a single morning in prayer. Would we even know what to do during an extended time of prayer? Would we fall asleep, or get bored and daydream, or use the time to think about other things or plan our coming week? Too often we think of prayer as just one-way communication with God, and we just don't have that much to say, especially since God knows everything anyway.

Or we may realize that prayer is two-way communication with God but fall prey to the fallacy that God speaks directly to us during prayer, so we just sit and wait for God to speak to us. Then we either get bored in the silence and go to sleep or else mistake our own thoughts for the words of God.

How God Speaks to Us Today

Prayer is clearly two-way communication with God, but today *God speaks to us through His Word.* Even in the days when God spoke directly to people, God's direct communication was rare and only to a select few, so people were encouraged to meditate and memorize whatever Scripture had already been revealed. Repeatedly the psalmist expressed the importance of meditating on God's Word while praying. Psalm 5:1,2 clearly shows the connection: "Give ear to my words, O Lord; consider my meditation. Hearken unto the voice of my cry, my King and my God, for unto thee will I pray" (KJV). The word used here for meditation is a word that has the idea of murmuring or muttering. The object of meditation is the person and work of God and His Word.

The vivid picture painted by this word "meditate" reminds us of our days in seminary when students were learning the basic verb and noun forms in Greek. We would write these down on index cards and carry them around in our pockets so that we could review them at any opportunity. We would take them out of our pocket to look at them, and then repeat them over and over to ourselves as we walked along. You can always spot the first-year language students at seminary because they are walking around muttering verb forms under their breath!

This is what we as believers are to do. As we pray without ceasing (1 Thessalonians 5:17) we are also meditating day and night (Psalm 1:2), praying God's Word back to Him and giving Him the tools He uses to work in our lives. The result of this continued meditation produces wisdom which guides us through life (Psalm 119:99). As the Word enters our souls, the Holy Spirit uses it to convict us of sin and shows us how to apply the Scriptures to our lives. Meditation also provides us with a knowledge of God's promises, which in turn reinforces and strengthens our prayer life as we learn more about what we should be praying for. If we are going to be effective in our prayers like Elijah, we must be often alone with God in prayer and meditation.

Persist in Prayer

We have already noticed that Elijah did not simply rest upon God's promise to provide rain, but when the time came he prayed for the rain to come. But when we look at that prayer we see that he prayed continually until the rain finally came. He began to pray, then sent his servant to see if the rain was coming. When it wasn't, he prayed again, and this went on seven times until finally a cloud began to appear. Elijah was effective in his prayer because, knowing the will of God, he was persistent.

Jesus emphasized this same point to His disciples when they asked Him to teach them how to pray. In Luke 11:5-10 He related the following illustration:

> Suppose one of you shall have a friend, and shall go to him at midnight and say to him, "Friend, lend me three loaves, for a friend of mine has come to me from a journey, and I have nothing to set before him"; and from inside he shall

> answer and say, "Do not bother me; the door has already been shut and my children and I are in bed; I cannot get up and give you anything." I tell you, even though he will not get up and give him anything because he is his friend, yet because of his persistence he will get up and give him as much as he needs. And I say to you, ask, and it shall be given to you; seek, and you shall find; knock, and it shall be opened to you. For everyone who asks receives, and he who seeks finds, and to him who knocks it shall be opened.

Jesus again emphasized this point in Luke 18:1-8. At that time He used the illustration of a widow coming for protection to a judge who neither feared nor respected God. At first he was unwilling, but he finally gave in because of her persistence. Jesus then made the point: "Shall not God bring about justice for His elect, who cry to Him day and night, and will He delay long over them?" (Luke 18:7). The point in both passages is that if sinful men are moved by persistence, how much more God will be.

However, mere persistence is not necessarily the basis for God answering our prayers. If something is not God's will for us, no matter how persistent we may be He will be even more persistent in saying no. An episode of this type is found in the life of the apostle Paul. In 2 Corinthians 12 Paul tells his readers that he was given a "thorn in the flesh, a messenger of Satan to buffet me" (verse 7). Even Paul came under demonic attack! How did he respond? He neither bound nor rebuked Satan. Instead he prayed! "Concerning this I entreated the Lord three times that it might depart from me" (verse 8). Though he prayed, God's answer was no. God said no because He had a reason for allowing the attack. It was to keep Paul humble, to teach him that God's grace was sufficient, and to teach him to persevere. Again we see that prayer and perseverance are linked together.

Strengthening God and Angels?

Some people claim that our persistence or lack of it strengthens or weakens God's ability to answer. Recent teaching among some groups of Christians has been that the angels that God uses to answer our prayers are strengthened to perform their task by the prayers of the saints, and if there are no prayers then the angels are weakened and become defeated in their combat with the demons. This approach views prayer as a great battery charger energizing the angels for action. While it is true that God uses the angels to carry out His answers to requests, nowhere is there any indication in the Bible that God's answers are determined by the prayers of the saints.

This is the same basic error prevalent among positive-confession advocates which places God in a position of obligation to man and puts the creature in a position of control over the Creator. This denies the clear biblical teaching of the sovereignty of God. God will certainly work out His purposes and plans for man and is not limited by the prayers of the saints.

The only passage we can find which someone might use to suggest that angels gain strength from the prayers of the saints is Daniel 10:12-21. Daniel had been praying for understanding from God for a period of three weeks, but no answer had come. During that time he continued to pray and to fast, but no answer came. Finally at the end of the third week an angel appeared in answer to his prayer. The reason it took three weeks was because he had been in combat with the "prince of the kingdom of Persia," a clear reference to the chief demon working to influence the government of Persia. Some may be tempted to think that it was Daniel's prayer and fasting that enabled the angel to persevere, but that is not what the Scripture says. The passage does not contain a cause/effect connection between Daniel's prayer and the angelic action. The angel who came to interpret Daniel's vision was clearly sent on the first day in response to the prayer, but the delay was because he was opposed by an evil angel. He was able to overcome the demon not because of Daniel's continued prayer and fasting but because Michael, "one of the chief princes of God," assisted him in winning the battle. Nowhere in this conflict is Daniel and his prayer in any way related to helping the angel get through to Daniel. All we see is the conflict and opposition viewed from below. To infer that Daniel's prayer helped the angel get through is illegitimate speculation.

Expecting Anwers

There was no doubt in Elijah's mind that God would bring rain. Because Elijah prayed on the promise of God, and because he knew the God behind the promises (since he had spent much time alone with God benefiting from His grace), and because he was persistent, he was completely confident in God's answer. When Elijah saw the small cloud in the sky on the edge of the horizon he turned to Ahab and warned him to hurry home so he would not get caught in the downpour. What a tremendous example of confidence!

This is the same attitude the believer is to have in his prayer life. Jesus told the disciples, "All things you ask in prayer, believing, you shall receive." (Matthew 21:22). We know from Scripture that without faith it is impossible to please God (Hebrews 11:6). This does not mean that God is obligated by our faith, but that in those areas where God desires to give us certain things, He withholds them because we do not trust Him. This is why James says, "You do not have because you do not ask" (4:2).

These four principles should govern our prayer lives: We should pray on the promises, we should cultivate a time for being alone with God, we should be persistent, and we should be confidently expectant.

Prayer is the communication lifeline of the believer. Just as a soldier behind enemy lines relies heavily on his radio to communicate with his support team, so the believer living in Satan's world must rely heavily upon prayer for his support team.

If we are going to be effective soldiers in our holy rebellion against Satan, we dare not allow ourselves to be cut off.

— 10 —

TRIUMPHANT WARRIORS

Therefore, since we have so great a cloud of witnesses surrounding us, let us also lay aside every encumbrance, and the sin which so easily entangles us, and let us run with endurance the race that is set before us, fixing our eyes on Jesus, the author and perfecter of faith.

—Hebrews 12:1,2

I (Thomas) remember the Saturday afternoon as if it were yesterday. When the phone rang it was one of my best friends, Gary. During the previous couple of years we had done much together—studied the Bible, prayed, worked, evangelized, traveled, and fellowshiped. Gary was the kind of guy who would give you the shirt off his back if you needed it, probably without having to ask.

I said hello to Gary and asked him what was up. Gary informed me that he just wanted to let me know he was quitting the Christian life. "WHAT?" I asked. "Quitting the Christian life?" "*Why*?" "I'm tired of confessing my sin," Gary replied. "But you don't just quit Christianity—it doesn't work that way!" I responded.

Unfortunately, Gary is just one example of many believers who start with a bang but then stray from the course. Some, like Gary, completely quit the race, while others just wander around in a state of spiritual confusion. Probably you also have friends who have followed a similar path. Why don't some Christians finish the race?

On the other hand, I also know believers who have endured even under great pressure. Some have had everything against them, humanly speaking, yet they continued to exhibit steady faith in the Lord Jesus Christ.

Anyone who is a fan of racing knows that mere speed is not enough to win races consistently. Effective contenders must also have *endurance* as well. Many auto races come down to a contest of who can stay in the race until the end. During a race a car may be knocked out of competition for various reasons. Some may blow an engine; others may crash into a wall or collide with other cars. A fire in the engine, electrical failure, or a flat tire can all lead to an early exit for a given contestant, even if he is leading the race at the moment. *Endurance* is a primary ingredient for any racer.

But endurance is a primary ingredient in the Christian life as well. What then are some of the roadblocks that a holy rebel will encounter in the marathon of the Christian life?

Suffering in a Feel-Good Society

We cannot think of a single instance of believers wanting to quit the Christian life that does not in some way relate to suffering. This is especially true in our modern, feel-good society: A person grows weary or is disappointed by what is required of him. Endurance, perseverance, and patience all require a person to suffer at some point, but suffering certainly does not feel good. As the writer of Hebrews put it, "All discipline for the moment seems not to be joyful, but sorrowful" (Hebrews 12:11). Therefore many Christians want to quit the race when they begin experiencing some pain or discomfort. The second half of Hebrews 12:11 goes on to say, "Yet to those who have been trained by it [discipline], afterwards it yields the peaceful fruit of righteousness." Suffering is an inevitable part of (though not all of) the Christian life. If suffering is not handled with endurance and faith, a believer will be tempted to drop out of the race.

Because suffering, if not properly understood and handled, often leads to an early exit from the race, we need to look at suffering from the perspective of God's Word. The Bible teaches that God, being good, did not directly create evil. Instead, evil entered the universe through God's rebellious creatures. However, now that evil has entered God's creation, He sovereignly uses evil for His own good purposes (Genesis 50:20; Exodus 3:18-20; Proverbs 16:4; Romans 8:28).[1] God is in control of all evil, and the suffering we experience in this life will be used by God to help us mature into Christlikeness.

The Ultimate Good

The greatest example of how God turns evil into good is seen in the death of Christ. First Corinthians 2:6-9 tells us that those involved in

---

1. Some of the material in this section, including reasons why Christians suffer, is adapted from Charles Clough, *Laying the Foundation* (Lubbock, TX: Lubbock Bible Church, 1973), pp. 64-66.

crucifying Christ did it out of an evil motive. However, Scripture also informs us that this was something "which God predestined before the ages to our glory" (1 Corinthians 2:7). The death of Christ resulted in the greatest of all blessings to mankind—our salvation from sin. Paul goes on to explain that God kept certain aspects of His plan a secret, because had the rulers of this age understood it, "they would not have crucified the Lord of glory" (1 Corinthians 2:8). This passage further explains that there are future blessings in the plan of God which He has not yet revealed, but which are going to be worth waiting for. The implication is that just because we cannot understand everything God is doing in our lives at the present time, including the suffering, this does not mean that God has no glorious purpose in store for us. The Bible teaches that there is a divine purpose behind all the suffering which evil brings upon God's children.

It is not as important to know in each case of suffering which of the above categories we fall into as it is to endure suffering with joy, hope, and endurance. Regardless of the purpose that God may have for specific events of suffering in our lives, we should handle each situation with the same Christian character. The future will reveal many of the specific reasons why we have suffered, as can be seen from the life of Job, but our calling in the present is to trust God to know what He is doing in our lives.

Scripture reveals at least four reasons why Christians suffer.

Reason One: Christians suffer because of the curse resulting from Adam's fall. Christians, and all humanity as well, suffer under God's curse upon creation as a result of the fall of Adam into sin (Genesis 3:8-24; Romans 5:12-21). This is the broadest purpose behind moral and physical evil and suffering. Those who have suffered the loss of a loved one (especially sudden and unexpected loss) or have been associated with someone with birth defects have experienced firsthand the effects resulting from Adam's fall. This kind of suffering and pain is not part of God's original creation, but is something resulting from man himself. Sometimes Christians realize this fact but still react bitterly toward God because He could have prevented the loss of a loved one, but did not, in their specific case. While it is true that God is gracious, we should also realize that God is also fair and just in His dealings with us. We just have to trust Him in these kinds of matters. Scripture recognizes the abnormality which Adam's sin has brought upon the human race and teaches that our only hope is in God's plan.

The pain related to the curse is noted in Romans 8:18-25. Paul contrasts "the sufferings of this present time" to "the glory that is to be revealed to us" in the future (verse 18). Why does humanity experience present suffering? Paul explains that it is due to Adam's fall (verses 20,21). The point of this passage is to let believers know that we have a hope for the future which will one day release us from the pain of present suffering. This is not something which is a hope for unbelievers, since their destiny is eternal suffering in the lake of fire. Because we have the hope of future glory and know that suffering and pain is only a temporary feature for the Christian, "with perseverance we wait eagerly for it" (verse 25). Paul is saying that the future hope of glory produces *perseverance* in the present life of a Christian.

Reason Two: God disciplines His children and uses adversity to produce godliness. This is probably one of the primary reasons for Christian suffering (Hebrews 12:3-15). When we respond to these experiences with patience, we learn what it means to be conformed to Christ (Colossians 1:24; James 1:2-4; 2 Peter 1:5-8). Anyone who has ever been involved in athletics knows that disciplined workouts are required, not because the coach is angry at his players, but because players must have a competent endurance level to compete in a game. The same is true of a soldier who is preparing for combat. Training in righteousness requires the tough exercise and discipline of learning to follow God's will instead of following our own selfish and often lustful feelings, regardless of the pain which may be involved in crucifying the flesh. But this kind of discipline produces the godly characteristic of perseverance needed to finish the race.

Reason Three: Some Christians suffer in a hostile world because we are identified with Christ. Jesus made this clear to His disciples in His farewell address to them in the upper room: "If the world hates you, you know that it has hated Me before it hated you. If you were of the world, the world would love its own; but because you are not of the world, but I chose you out of the world, therefore the world hates you" (John 15:18,19). People who have not trusted Christ as their Savior from their sins have an innate animosity toward Christ and His people when they are challenged about their relationship to God. Often they take out their hatred toward Christ on His messengers. Christ is telling His holy rebels that we can expect this type of response. It is in a sense normal that the world responds this way, so we should not be surprised when it occurs. Our goal should be to respond to this kind of suffering the way the early disciples did as recorded in Acts 5:41: "They went on their way from the presence of the Council, rejoicing that they had been considered worthy to suffer shame for His name."

Reason Four: Christians sometimes suffer in order to be a testimony to all creation of God's grace. This is a testimony to angels (Ephesians 3:10), other Christians (2 Corinthians 1:3-6; 4:8-12), and non-Christians (1 Peter 2:12-20; 3:13-17). When we respond to suffering and hardship in a proper manner it can be an encouragement to other believers of the grace of God in the life of believers. We can be an encouragement and not a detriment to others, as Paul explains: "If we are afflicted, it is for your comfort and salvation; or if we are comforted, it is for your comfort, which is effective in the patient enduring of the same sufferings which we also suffer" (2 Corinthians 1:6).

In addition to encouraging other believers, we learn from Ephesians 3:10 that angels ("the rulers and the authorities in the heavenly places") are learning lessons "through the church." What lessons do they learn? Ephesians 3:4-7 indicates that they are learning as history unfolds about God's grace as expressed in Christ. The angelic realm cannot personally experience saving grace, so they must learn about it from believers in Christ.

Non-Christians are part of the "all creation" cited in Reason Four. When non-Christians observe the way Christians handle suffering, this can be a testimony to them of Jesus Christ working in our lives. First Peter 3:17 says, "That you suffer for doing what is right rather than for doing what is wrong." In this way "those who revile your good behavior in Christ may be put to shame" (3:16). Unbelievers often watch believers who have spoken out for Christ to see how He has affected our lives. What better testimony to the world than the way we handle adversity and suffering? Perseverance, endurance, and patience are the biblical response of the Christian to suffering.

Suffering God's Way

Christians can learn much about the nature of perseverance by understanding the Greek word for perseverance in the New Testament. The verb *hupomeno* is made up of two smaller Greek words: *hupo*, meaning "under," and *meno*, meaning "to remain." Taken together, they mean "to remain under." Remain under what? It depends on what the word is referring to. If it is talking about the sufferings related to trials, as in 1 Peter 2:20, "when you do what is right and suffer for it you patiently endure it, this finds favor with God," then perseverance, endurance, or patience refers to the ability to remain under the pressure of a given situation rather than seeking to escape it for the temporary relief from the pain of suffering.

How does this apply to the issue of spiritual warfare? Some deliverance teachers say that many of our problems and trials can be dealt with by simply rebuking Satan, and then these trials will be instantly removed from a believer's life. This is very appealing to many modern Christians who have grown up in a society where we don't have to wait very long for anything. However, this is not the way God normally works. In the first place, many of our problems stem from the flesh. Therefore God wants us to learn how to resist sin in our lives through the often-painful process of learning to trust Him to overcome these problems. The red herring of instant relief from our trials does not lend itself to the development of patience in our trials. It is the lessons learned from "remaining under" the pressure of a given situation which produce Christlike character in our lives. This is what Paul means in Romans 5:3,4 when he tells us that "we also exult in our tribulations, knowing that tribulation brings about perseverance; and perseverance, proven character; and proven character, hope."

Rebuking the Devil?

Many people are being led astray by deliverance teachings which promise instantaneous victory over one's problems by a timely rebuke of the devil. This misleads people from the biblical path of exercising endurance or patience in meeting their trials. As a result, many believers are not developing the kind of proven character they need to handle trials.

This character-building approach is illustrated by Paul's thorn in the flesh (2 Corinthians 12:7-10). The thorn is described as "a messenger of Satan to buffet me—to keep me from exalting myself" (12:7). It is possible this messenger was a demon. The Greek word for messenger is *angelos*, the word for angel. This kind of situation is often viewed by deliverance teachers today as something which is not in keeping with the will of God, and they would seek to rebuke this "messenger of Satan" and run him out of town by giving him two black eyes in the process. But this was not Paul's response. Instead, he "entreated the Lord three times that it might depart from me" (12:8). Yet God did not grant Paul's request. But don't we have power in the name of Jesus? Yes, we do, but it is to be exercised within the will of God. The Lord was more interested in building Christlike character in Paul as a true display of His power (12:9) than in putting on the kind of fireworks display which many today are calling "power encounters."

Within certain circles today it is common to hear a speaker lash out against Satan with various rebukes. Often the speaker will rebuke Satan in the area of health, wealth, and peace of mind. It is not unusual to hear more preaching against Satan and the demonic than to hear preaching on Christ and His resources. Many people become so concerned with what the devil is doing that they take their eyes off the Lord.

We must realize that believers are never instructed to rebuke the devil or his demons. The New Testament views rebuking as the sole prerogative of Jesus as an expression of His lordship and sovereignty over the spirit realm.[2] The only acceptable condition for a believer to rebuke is when he lovingly corrects a brother fallen into sin (Luke 17:3; 1 Timothy 5:20). Throughout the New Testament rebuke is understood as the sole prerogative of the Lord, and this is why Michael said when challenged by Satan, "The Lord rebuke you" (Jude 9).

Marks of a False Prophet

Second Peter 2 describes and denounces false prophets who will be active within the church until the second coming of Christ. Peter exposes their self-centered motives and conduct in the first three verses and then pronounces their condemnation (verses 4-9). The rest of the chapter concludes with a description of their characteristics. One characteristic that the contemporary church would do well to take note of is found in verse 10: "Especially those who indulge the flesh in its corrupt desire and despise authority. Daring, self-willed, they do not tremble when they revile angelic majesties." The earlier context indicates that these self-willed false prophets were engaged in reviling fallen angelic majesties—demons. Remember that this is something which is characteristic of false prophets, so it is a warning for Christians not to engage in such practices.

---

2. Gerhard Kittle, ed., *Theological Dictionary of the New Testament, Vol. 2* (Grand Rapids: Eerdmans, 1964), pp. 625-26.

Peter goes on to explain this practice in greater detail in verses 11 and 12. He notes that "angels who are greater in might and power do not bring a reviling judgment against them before the Lord" (verse 11). Angels know better than to do such foolish things as rebuking or reviling other angels. They have much greater strength and power than the greatest human being, yet they know better than to engage in such practices. Certainly God's holy angels cannot be justly accused of not being involved in spiritual warfare, but for them, as it should be for us, it is a question of being properly involved.

Jude 8,9, in a similar warning about false teachers, gives a specific example of this kind of incident. Jude uses almost identical language when he notes that the false teachers "defile the flesh, and reject authority, and revile angelic majesties" (verse 8). How do they do that? He tells us that "Michael the archangel, when he disputed with the devil and argued about the body of Moses, did not dare pronounce against him a railing judgment, but said, 'The Lord rebuke you'" (verse 9). This passage is telling us that even Michael, the highest-ranking elect angel, would not rebuke the devil; yet many Christians today do it on a regular basis. The text says "did not dare," which means that doing such a thing was so unthinkable for Michael that he would not even come close to doing such a thing. Michael did not even say what we hear many people saying today: "I rebuke you, devil, in the name of the Lord!" Michael simply said, "The Lord rebuke you." Unlike many modern Christians, Michael knew that rebuking was a prerogative of the Lord alone!

With not *one*, but *two* warnings in Scripture against such practices the question must be asked, "Why do so many Christians and Christian leaders regularly engage in such practices?" Both passages give us the answer: They are acting out of ignorance. "These, like unreasoning animals... reviling where they have no knowledge..." (2 Peter 2:12). "These men revile the things which they do not understand..." (Jude 10).

This is an example of ignorance of God's Word leading to wrong practice in the area of spiritual warfare. No wonder many Christians are growing weary and dropping out of the battle! Many are following leaders who are leading them on wild-goose chases through beliefs and practices that open them up to *attacks* from the enemy rather than the advertised protection from the enemy. A holy rebel can develop true maturity only through genuine biblical training, which teaches us to keep our eyes upon Christ and not be preoccupied with the demonic.

Training for the Big Game

The Book of Hebrews was written to Jewish believers who had trusted Christ as their Savior. As time passed some were starting to "drift away" (2:1) from Christ back into the comfort and familiarity of Judaism. The writer of Hebrews demonstrates the error of this thinking by showing that the old (Judaism) was merely temporary and looked forward to the fulfillment in Jesus the Messiah. Jesus the Messiah fulfilled the shadows of Old Testament ritual in His ministry. Therefore five warning passages are issued to the Jewish readers showing that if they grow impatient with Christ and His work, a return to the old way will lead only to judgment, since then they have no Messiah who actually took away sin. After showing that the new things in Christ are superior to the old things in Judaism, the writer of Hebrews notes how the saints from the Old Testament never received these promises in their lifetimes, but faithfully continued in their trust of God (Hebrews 11). By the time the writer gets to Hebrews 12 he is telling the Hebrews, and us, that if their brethren displayed such faith and endurance without having seen Jesus the Messiah, their faith should be even greater, since they, and we, are able to look back to Jesus as our example. This forms the context for understanding Hebrews 12.

A good friend of ours was a pro football player who was a starter on a winning Super Bowl team. He told us how this is the ultimate test for a pro athlete, since the importance and national interest of such a game provides a powerful incentive for any player to prepare and perform at his best. A similar picture is painted in the first two verses of Hebrews 12. The stands are packed with "so great a cloud of witnesses surrounding us" (12:1), which are the Old Testament saints from chapter 11. The players are readying themselves by laying "aside every encumbrance, and the sin which so easily entangles us" (12:1). The hindrances in the race are said to be sin generated by each believer, not external demonic attacks. The resolve carried into the contest consists of running the race "with endurance" (12:1). The Christian life is not a sprint, but a marathon that requires endurance, which in turn requires training and resolve.

The Right Example

Hebrews 12:2 pictures the runner in the starting blocks fixing his eyes on Jesus. On *Jesus*, not on Satan and the demonic! *Christ* is our example because He has run the race before us and is the model of how to properly run the race. Three things furnished Christ's motivation and should be ours as well. First, He emphasized "the joy set before Him." His orientation was not on the present pain of the race but on the joy which would result when He finished the race. He was *future*-oriented, not present-oriented. Second, He "endured the cross." He did not let the suffering aspect of His mission knock Him out of the race because of His future orientation. Third, He was "despising the shame." The world viewed His death as a shame, an embarrassment. But Christ despised that. When He endured and finished the race He "sat down at the right hand of the throne of God." The glory comes after we have endured the pain of the race; then we are able to sit down and receive the glory.

Next we are told to "consider Him who has endured such hostility by sinners against Himself, so that you may not grow weary and lose heart" (12:3). "Consider" means to contemplate, to think about. In context it implies that we are to sit down and think through a strategy which will enable us to successfully run this race of endurance. How are we to develop the character and internal fortitude to complete such a race? By modeling our own race strategy after the one run by Christ. There is a twofold purpose for this. The first purpose is that we "may not grow weary" or become discouraged. This often happens to a runner who starts a long race. Early in the race he begins to realize that this is going to be a long, tough haul, and soon he becomes discouraged and begins to think about dropping out of the race. The second purpose is that we may not lose heart or suffer from low morale. This could also lead to dropping out of the race.

Over the last few years we have talked with many Christians who have become discouraged with the "quick fix" approaches to spiritual warfare in which they were taught to *rebuke* Satan rather than *resist* him in order to handle their problems. When this strategy didn't work, they become discouraged and dropped by the wayside. Often these people didn't really want to quit the race, but simply had not received the proper training or developed the kind of maturity and character necessary to endure the tough battles. Their basic problem is that they had been on a spiritual diet of ice cream and cookies and their exercise program had amounted to watching games on television while relaxing in their easy chair.

Hebrews 12 goes on to speak of the need to develop discipline and maturity in our lives if we are to properly complete the race, as those in the stands have already done. This training "yields the peaceful fruit of righteousness" (12:11). Godly character takes time to develop through practice and discipline.

Helping the Weak

When I (Thomas) was in Army boot camp we often went on long marches. Our goal was for the whole company to successfully complete the march. If one man dropped out, then we did not complete our mission. Therefore the strong were encouraged to help the weak by carrying their pack or helping them make it to the finish so that the company as a whole could make it to the finish line. Likewise some Christians are stronger than others, and we are admonished in the New Testament to help those within the body of Christ who are weak. What is the cause of weakness, according to the New Testament? Repeatedly it is said to be sin in a person's life which has not been properly dealt with. Such sin hinders a Christian's spiritual development, rendering him spiritually weak (Hebrews 12:1).

The danger we face is to grow weary in the struggle. The writer to the Hebrews exhorts us to consider Jesus so that we will not grow weary and lose heart. The Greek word for weary here occurs in two other important passages, Revelation 2:3 and James 5:15. In both the Hebrews and Revelation passages it is clear that the word is used in contrast to endurance. The same is true in the James passage. Unfortunately, the passage has traditionally been understood as teaching something about healing physical sickness. We recognize that this is a debated passage, but when properly understood and applied, we believe that it offers great hope to the believer whose endurance is failing.

Can All Illness Be Healed?

Many people have struggled with the traditional explanation of James 5:13-16, which focuses on physical sickness. The reason for this struggle is that verse 15, "the prayer offered in faith will restore the one who is sick," appears to be an unconditional promise but often seems to be unfulfilled.

On July 7, 1952, my mother (Robert) was stricken with polio. I was born less than a month later, and have never seen my mother walk. When I was a child, with the faith of a child, I regularly prayed that God would heal her so that she could walk again. This prayer was never answered. Later I came to realize that God does not always answer a prayer for healing. However, James 5:15, if it is talking about physical disease, indicates that God will always heal. Another well-known case of God's not healing someone is that of Joni Earickson Tada. She writes that many Christians have prayed for her, anointed her with oil, and laid hands on her, yet she is still a quadriplegic to the glory of God. In light of these and many other situations where God has not healed, we must be open to the possibility that this passage may not be talking about physical healing at all, but spiritual healing instead. We all recognize that many people we pray for who are sick never recover and even die. Is this because we lack faith, or that God is not faithful? Or could it be that the sickness mentioned here is something other than physical illness?

The word translated "sick" in verse 14 ("Is anyone among you sick?") has two meanings in the Greek. At its root is the idea of *weakness*. In some places the weakness is physical (Matthew 10:8; Luke 4:40; John 4:46) and in others the weakness is spiritual (Romans 6:19; 8:26; 2 Corinthians 12:5,9,10). It is the *context* that determines whether the meaning is spiritual or physical. In James 5 two different Greek words are translated "sick." The first is in verse 14 and translates the Greek *asthenes*. The next verse translates the Greek word *kamno* as "sick." Since *kamno* clearly means to be spiritually weary (Hebrews 12:3; Revelation 2:3), we learn that James did not have *physical* weakness in mind, but *spiritual* weakness.

This is further supported by the fact that the entire thrust of James, and especially this last chapter, is on patience (5:7,8,10) and endurance (5:11). The example used by James to illustrate his point is from the Old Testament, when Elijah persevered in his confrontation with Ahab (1 Kings 17:1). If James were talking about healing a *physical* disease, that same chapter in 1 Kings provides a much better illustration: Elijah restoring life to the widow's son.

There are excellent biblical grounds for understanding this passage to be talking about what to do if and when a believer is growing weary. First, he is to lean upon more mature believers and their prayers. He is to call upon the elders to have them pray for him. Further, if there is sin in his life, sin that entangles him and destroys his endurance, he is to confess that sin (James 5:16). The result is that he will be "healed." Again we find that the original Greek here is found in our other endurance passage, Hebrews 12. There we find the writer concluding his exhortation to endurance by saying, "Therefore strengthen the hands that are weak and the knees that are feeble, and make straight paths for your feet, so that the limb which is lame may not be put out of joint, but rather be healed" (verses 12,13). It is clear from the context that the writer is using a physical-healing figure of speech to describe what must take place in the body of Christ when a brother or sister is weary of the struggle: He must be lifted up; he must lean on the stronger Christian; he must be strengthened in his faith.

The Scriptures are consistent in stating that the solution to struggle in the Christian life is based on prayer—a recognition of our submission to God and reliance upon His strength rather than ours. We need to confess and turn from sin in our lives as we move toward obedience to the truth. When we are weak we should cry out to God, as David did many times as recorded in the Psalms. We should also seek the counsel of more mature Christians to encourage and help us along the way, as we have seen in James 5.

Patience in Action

As we have already seen, the Epistle of James has much to say about patience and endurance. James begins his letter with the admonition to be joyful through trials because this produces endurance in the life of the faithful believer (1:2-4). Toward the end of the epistle James returns to the theme of endurance or patience and cites three examples of patient endurance needed to handle our trials (5:7-11). Some of us may be happy to know that there are limits on how long believers are expected to patiently endure; we only have to be patient "until the coming of the Lord" (5:7). After that event the race is over, and patience and endurance will no longer be required of Christians.

The first example of patient endurance is illustrated by the farmer who has to wait on rain in order for his crop to grow into a harvest (5:7,8). Then the Old Testament prophets are presented as "an example, brethren, of suffering and patience . . . who spoke in the name of the Lord" (5:10). These men had to suffer during their lifetime for giving a prophecy which would not be fulfilled in their lifetime. This took patient endurance. James also reminds us, "You have heard of the endurance of Job and have seen the outcome of the Lord's dealings, that the Lord is full of compassion and is merciful" (5:11). Job had to trust God to vindicate him and bless him even though he was engaged in one of the most severe attacks from Satan in the history of the world. So the life of Job is a model of a believer handling a satanic attack with endurance and patience. Now let's look at what occasioned Satan's encounter with Job.

The Patience of Job

When I (Thomas) was a teenager, a group of us would pile into a car and go cruising. This is still a common activity for many young people who are looking for potential excitement. In the first chapter of Job, the Bible tells us that Satan does some cruising of his own, and that God gives even Satan access to His presence (Job 1:6). Much of his time is spent cruising the earth looking for rebels without a cause.

When God asked Satan, "From where do you come?" Satan replied, "From roaming about on the earth and walking around on it" (1:7). The Hebrew word translated "roaming" is used to describe the way a lion would roam an area looking for his prey. When the lion would locate a potential victim, he would stalk his prey and at just the right time move in for the kill. This is the same description used to describe Satan's activities when the Lord asked him about a certain individual—Job. "Have you considered My servant Job?" the Lord challenged. Apparently Satan had, because he shot back, "Does Job fear God for nothing?" Today we might say something like, "He's only in it for the money." But in order to demonstrate that Job served God because he loved God for who He is and not just for the benefits that Sugar Daddy provides, God allowed Satan to attack him to such a severe degree that the very name "Job" has become synonymous with undeserved suffering down through history, even in our own day.

The apostle Peter must have had the Job passage in mind when the Holy Spirit moved him to picture Satan, the devil, as one who "prowls about like a roaring lion, seeking someone to devour" (1 Peter 5:8). What did Peter prescribe for the believer in light of Satan's persistent harassments? We are to be persistent in our fight against him. Peter says that the hard times which Satan puts us through do not result in aid to Satan's cause; instead, godly resistance to Satan produces Christlike character and maturity, giving a battle-tested stability to our lives (1 Peter 5:9-11).

Response for Holy Rebels

How does Peter instruct a holy rebel to react to Satan's attacks? Not by talking about how we are going to run the devil out of town or give him a black eye or even two black eyes. Scripture says that we are to *resist* him (1 Peter 5:9). The same command is given in James 4:7 and Ephesians 6:11,13,14. This is what the Bible specifically and repeatedly says is to be our strategy when Satan attacks us. Scripture does not tell us to develop from experience a formula of rebuking, binding, insulting, or arguing with Satan and the demonic. Instead, we are to follow God's explicit instructions on this issue. By habitually following God's Word we will see the Lord bring stability and character into our lives, including the type of endurance that we need in order to engage in spiritual warfare without fainting in the day of battle.

– 11 –

War's End

I saw an angel coming down from heaven, having the key of the abyss and a great chain in his hand. And he laid hold of the dragon, the serpent of old, who is the devil and Satan, and bound him for a thousand years, and threw him into the abyss, and shut it and sealed it over him, so that he should not deceive the nations any longer, until the thousand years were completed;

—Revelation 20:1-3

After Satan led a rebellion against God in which he recruited one-third of the angels and all of mankind, God launched a counterattack by enlisting holy rebels from Adam's descendants, those whom He has called out from the darkness of our sin to be a part of His coming kingdom. The battle involving the eternal destiny of humanity is rapidly moving toward its grand climax. Even though Satan and his company are a defeated foe as a result of Christ's work on the cross, the war is still being played out, with some of the hottest battles yet to come. How will the war end, and what significance does that hold for holy rebels today?

The Two-Stage Conquest

God's victory over Satan is being worked out in two stages. *Stage one* was accomplished on the cross. At that point Satan's defeat was sure, his destiny certain. But defeated though he was, he still has power to operate, so much so that he is still called the "god of this age" (2 Corinthinans 4:4). His ultimate defeat will be accomplished in *stage two*, during the second coming of Christ. At this time Satan will be defeated and bound in the bottomless pit for 1000 years, after which he will be released for a short while, to be defeated again and thrown into the lake of fire for eternity (Revelation 20:1-3,10).

Since we live in the interim period between stages one and two, called the church age, we must determine what our strategy toward

Satan should be. We have seen that in the current church age we as believers are to engage in spiritual warfare *defensively* by standing against Satan. We do this solely on the basis of our position in Christ, which was gained for us by Christ at His first coming, when His humiliation brought about the forgiveness of our sins. Ultimate victory will be accomplished at His second coming, when in glory He will sweep Satan and his demons from the field of play and remove them from the realm of human activity. In the meantime His holy rebels are to remain faithful in their defensive position, standing firm in the faith.

The defensive posture toward Satan and his demons appears to have been part of God's plan for His creatures even before the fall of man. God told Adam to subdue and rule over the *earth* (Genesis 1:26), not the heavens. When God placed man in the Garden He told him to cultivate and keep it (Genesis 2:15). Many Bible scholars have pointed out that the word for "keep" includes the idea of guarding. The implication is that Adam was to guard against an intrusion, which we know from Genesis 3 was Satan. Man as God's creature has always been in the position of defending himself with God's Word. It appears that for a creature to go on the offensive against Satan is to usurp a divine perogative reserved for God alone. The creature's posture is trust in God by taking a defensive stance.

Wrong Strategy

The last decade has seen the rise of many people teaching that the church of Jesus Christ is to take up an *offensive* strategy against Satan and the demonic before Christ returns. This error is the result of a poor understanding of God's purpose for this age and the age to come, as well as a failure to distinguish the threefold aspect of Satan's defeat. From the earliest times in history, Satan has attempted to deceive God's people into doing something which is good (in this case launching out on an offensive attack against Satan and the demonic) by engaging in it wrongly or prematurely. Satan tempted Adam and Eve with a promise of knowledge, something they would have received from God anyway had they slowed down and gone about it God's way. However, they believed they could have it when they wanted it, and this resulted in humanity being cast into sin. Satan later unsuccesssfully tempted Christ with the kingdoms of this world, something that Christ will end up with anyway (Revelation 11:15).

In a military briefing, I (Tommy) was once told how Russian offensive strategy is to attack in three waves. The first wave would strike out and initiate the attack. The second and third waves were held in reserve, waiting for the time when the battle would become fierce and the momentum of the attack was being slowed. The Americans have countered with a strategy, because of our inferior numbers, which is designed to make the Russians think that they have met large pockets of resistance which necessitate deployment of the second and third waves prematurely. This strategy of premature deployment is designed to trick the Russians into expending their energy and resources in fighting a phantom enemy. Then when they have spent themselves, the Americans can move in and exact a fatal blow. This is similar to what Satan is attempting to do to Christians who attempt to go on the offensive before our General—Jesus Christ—has decided on such a plan.

When Satan tricks Christians into expending their time and energy in wrong directions, he has achieved a temporary victory, and that is why it is important to know how the war will end. It will end during the final seven years of history (the tribulation period) with a series of the most spectacular events the world will ever see. Part of those events will include direct combat between Jesus Christ and Satan, as well as battles between the holy angels and the demons. Jesus Christ will be victorious. It is only by understanding this fact that we can live effectively today as holy rebels and avoid being duped by Satan into premature deployment. As holy rebels we must not fall into the trap (as many people within the church are doing today) of substituting Satan's strategy for God's.

Two major errors are being advocated today which often lead to improper strategies in spiritual warfare. The first type of error relates to the *means* of our spiritual warfare, which we have already discussed at length. The second type of error relates to the *timing* of Christ's ultimate victory, which we will explain in the rest of this chapter.

Binding Satan and Demons?

In Chapter 6 we dealt extensively with this error, but we will mention it again to further drive home the point that this is an error relating to *timing*, as well as means. First, the *time* when Satan and the demons will be bound is in the *future*, not in present, as Revelation 20:2 tells us: "He laid hold of . . . Satan, and bound him for a thousand years." Our present strategy is prescribed by the Bible as resisting him (Ephesians 6:11; James 4:7; 1 Peter 5:9). Second, God will not be using believers to round up Satan and put him out of commission by binding. Instead, the *means* that God will use is stated clearly in Revelation 20:1, where it says that "an *angel* coming down from heaven, having the key of the abyss and a great chain in his hand," will do the honors. Therefore the idea that believers have removed Satan and his demon armies from spheres of influence because they have prayed for Satan's binding is unbiblical.

Inherited Curses?

This error of timing misinterprets Scripture from a past era and wrongly applies it to present circumstances. It is the view that occult powers or curses are passed from parent to child. Those advocating this view usually quote from Exodus 20:5: "You shall not worship them or serve them; for I, the Lord your God, am a jealous God, visiting the iniquity of the fathers on the children, on the third and the fourth generations of those who hate Me." Proponents of this view believe that if a parent's or grandparent's curse or occult power is not specifically uncovered and removed by renouncing it, a Christian can be oppressed by such a past curse.

There are at least two reasons why this view is an inaccurate application of the passage. First, when a person becomes a Christian he is delivered from all his sins, including his occult sin, since a Christian cannot be demon-possessed. *The Bible does not recognize occult sin as a special category of sin that has not been dealt with by the cross.* Remember that everyone is born under the authority of Satan (Colossians 1:13) and has Satan working through him (Ephesians 2:2). Second, it is wrong to assume that Exodus 20:5 refers to God's "visiting the iniquity of the fathers on the children" because of *inheritance* rather than because each successive generation decides to follow in the footsteps of their parents. Ezekiel 18:2-20 says that God curses each Israelite individual for his *own* sins and not specifically because of something that his fathers may have done. God specifically states in verse 4 that "all souls are Mine; the soul of the father as well as the soul of the son is mine." God goes on to state that if the son does right, in contrast to the parents' sins, including occult sins, then "he shall surely live."

This kind of "I-inherited-it-from-my-parents" view is also a popular explanation for all kinds of aberrant behavior within many Christian psychology circles as well. It is used to explain mental and emotional disease, chronic sickness, all sorts of female problems from miscarriage to PMS, marriage and financial problems, rebellious teenagers, etc. But the idea that a Christian might have to be delivered specifically from a curse or occult power which salvation in Christ has not taken care of is not found in Scripture. In fact *there is not one example in the entire Bible of a saved person being under a satanic curse which had to be broken by Christian exorcism or distinct confession.* The only curses which the Bible treats as effective are those uttered by God. This attempt to shift responsibility for current failures to someone else is reminiscent of Adam's attempt to shift the blame for his sin to Eve.

Other deliverance teachers say that any Christian with an occult past must specifically renounce those sins or else he will not be free. In other words, he must have a separate, postsalvation deliverance from occult sins. Yet if this is true, then Christ's work really did not forgive us of all our sins. If this is true, then we would need to specifically go back and name all our sins in order to be saved. But this is completely contrary to the entire teaching of Scripture that Christ dies for all sin—past, present, and future— and that we are forgiven and delivered from all our sins at the point of salvation.

Regarding this "curses" approach, Dr. John Hannah makes the following perceptive comment:

> Christians do face demonic opposition, for which God has provided the appropriate spiritual armor (Ephesians 6:10 ff.). We must put it on and utilize it to the fullest extent. However, we do *not* need some additional procedure for dealing with evil curses, for which there is no scriptural warrant. This is a mixture of Christianity with Zoroastrianism, Eastern mysticism, and black magic *voodoo*). We do well to remember the old fable of the "tar baby and the rabbit"![1]

Dominion Theology

The 1980's saw the rise of the idea that since we are in the kingdom right now, we should take dominion over Christ's enemies, in essence

1. John David Hannah, "The 'Curses' Syndrome—An Evaluation," unpublished paper delivered at the Evangelical Minister's Fellowship, Houston, Texas, Spring 1985, p. 3.

running them out of town.[2] This thinking has been around for a long time, but it has become dominant in many circles today. This error stems from the wrong view that we are currently in the kingdom/ millennium instead of the church age. Once again, characteristics of the future are confused with those of the present. Those who hold this view suggest that since Satan and the demons will be gone during the kingdom, it is the church's responsibility to take the offensive and "run them out of town." We are told that if we will do this, territories which have been under the control of demons and evil spirits will be liberated, and this will greatly facilitate evangelism, social reform, and godly political progress.

This could be viewed as something similar to Christian ghostbusters. If there is something weird in your neighborhood, and if you know the right group to call, you can exterminate your neighborhood of demons and evil spirits. With the devil and his crowd out of town, then you can get down to the important business of solving the world's problems. Whatever happened to simply preaching the gospel and trusting God the Holy Spirit to do His work?

The April 1990 issue of *Charisma* magazine featured cover stories on how to defeat "territorial spirits." John Dawson, author of a new book, *Taking Our Cities for God*, contributed an article entitled "Winning the Battle for Your Neighborhood: How you can drive away the demon forces now dominating the streets where you live."[3] Steven Lawson wrote on the subject "Defeating Territorial Spirits: Battles against evil spiritual forces controlling our cities can be waged and won."[4] Lawson gave many examples of dealing with territorial spirits, usually along the lines that a Christian ministry was ineffective in a particular area until the Christians tuned into the fact that territorial demons were in control. Once they did battle, they were able to identify these strongholds and force them to give up their territory. They claim this resulted in the outbreak of spiritual revival.

C. Peter Wagner of Fuller Seminary's School of World Mission sees the defeating of territorial spirits as central to fulfilling Christ's Great

---

2. For critiques of these movements see H. Wayne House and Thomas Ice, *Dominion Theology: Blessing or Curse?* (Portland: Multnomah Press, 1988); Hal Lindsey, *The Road to Holocaust* (New York: Bantam Books, 1989); Dave Hunt, *Whatever Happened to Heaven?* (Eugene, OR: Harvest House, 1988); Albert James Dager, *Vengeance Is Ours: The Church in Dominion* (Sword Publishers, 1990).
3. John Dawson, *Charisma*, April 1990, p. 57.
4. Steven Lawson, *Charisma*, April 1990, p. 47.

Commission. Wagner suggests that certain countries like Japan, which have had a low response rate to the gospel compared with similar countries, could be bound by territorial spirits. If some brave soul could discern the location and nature of these spirits, and break their stronghold, then it could lead to a harvest of souls in Japan.[5]

While it is certainly true that there is organization within the demonic realm (Ephesians 6:12), it does not follow from this fact or any other biblical evidence that demons can interfere with our sovereign God's work of evangelism. God can save His elect through the preaching of the gospel no matter what the spiritual climate. He is sovereign! In addition, the idea that we can run these so-called "territorial demons" out of town is based on an error in timing. This kind of offensive tactic is invalid during the church age, which is a time when God is "taking from among the Gentiles a people for His name" (Acts 15:14). The offensive defeat of Satan and the demonic is something that awaits the end times, and will be accomplished not by Christians but by Christ Himself and His holy angels. This kind of dominion teaching impatiently confuses God's defensive strategy for His holy rebels during this age with the offensive strategy of Christ and His angels during the age to come.

Restoration Teaching

Another teaching coming from dominion theology is the idea that the Lord cannot and will not return until the body of Christ has reached some kind of unity, which will contribute to increased power within the church, thereby leading to the greatest revival the world has ever seen. Sometimes related to these views is the idea that Christians must submit to certain leaders and their teachings so that they will have phenomenal power and influence when apostolic Christianity is restored and the revival of the "latter rain" begins, probably by the year 2000.

Many of these teachings sprang up in the late 1940's through Pentecostals such as Franklin Hall and William Branham, and were disseminated from meetings held at Sharon Orphanage and Schools in North Battleford, Saskatchewan, in early 1948. The leading Pentecostal denomination, the Assemblies of God, declared these and

---

5. C. Peter Wagner and F. Douglas Pennoger, eds., *Wrestling with Dark Angels* (Ventura, CA: Regal Books, 1990), p. 89.

other teachings steming from that source to be heresy, and the movement died down for a while. But in the last few years many bits and pieces of these teachings are strongly surfacing again.[6]

Many of the teachings are based upon alleged revelations received by various leaders in the movement who are considered to be prophets and apostles. Unfortunately, when they try to support their views from Scripture, they repeatedly take passages which refer to God's unfulfilled future restoration and blessing of Israel in the last days and wrongly apply it to the church. Acts 3:19-21 is an example of their misunderstanding of the *timing* for the fulfillment of that passage. Shortly after the Day of Pentecost, Peter preached a second major sermon to the Jews in Jerusalem showing that Jesus was their promised Messiah. He concluded with an explanation that only when Israel (not the church) received Jesus as their Messiah would the promised kingdom come:

> Repent therefore and return, that your sins may be wiped away, in order that times of refreshing may come from the presence of the Lord, and that He may send Jesus, the Christ appointed for you, whom heaven must receive until the period of restoration of all things about which God spoke by the mouth of His holy prophets from ancient time.

It is important that certain key phrases are properly understood in the context in which Peter spoke them. "Times of refreshing" (verse 19) is a description of the millennial kingdom promised to Israel in the Old Testament. This time would come when Israel accepted their Messiah (Matthew 23:37-39; Zechariah 12:10). The "period of restoration of all things" (verse 21) is a term used by the Old Testament prophets to refer to the restoration of Israel at the end times (Jeremiah 15:19; 16:15; 24:6; 50:19; Ezekiel 16:55; Hosea 11:11). Nowhere does the Bible speak of the church ever being restored. The Bible reveals nothing of a great revival, a latter-day rainstorm, which will be produced by a "perfected" body of Christ or some kind of restoration of a "superspiritual" brand of Christianity shortly before Christ's second coming. The New Testament does not comment directly one way or the other about an increased or decreased rate of conversion at

---

6. See Albert James Dager, "Latter-Day Prophets: The Kansas City Connection," *Media Spotlight* 1990 (P.O. Box 290, Redmond, WA 98073). See also Thomas Ice, "What is Dominion Theology?" *Biblical Perspectives*, Vol. I, No. 3, May/June 1988 (P.O. Box 90014, Austin, TX 78709).

any point in the church age. However, it *does* teach that there will be increasing apostasy as the age progresses (2 Timothy 3:1-17), hardly an environment which is produced by a church in revival!

Much of the false teaching related to the restoration-and-overcomer teachings lie behind the contemporary teaching about spiritual warfare. This teaching often revolves around the theme that you need the special teaching which a given teacher or ministry espouses in order to defeat Satan and the demonic so that you can become one of God's special end-time warriors.

Colossians 2:18 warns believers about getting involved in "the worship of the angels, taking his stand on visions he has seen, inflated without cause by his fleshly mind." It is because we are in a spiritual warfare and the demonic is real that we take seriously the Bible's sober warnings against falling prey to false doctrine being propagated by "false apostles, deceitful workers, disguising themselves as apostles of Christ" (2 Corinthians 11:13). True biblical discernment is an essential ingredient required of faithful holy rebels.

Doctrines of Demons

Paul warns believers in 1 Timothy 4:1:

> The Spirit explicitly says that in later times some will fall away from the faith, paying attention to deceitful spirits and doctrines of demons.

What does the phrase "later times" mean? It very likely refers to the "later times" of the current church age. Notice that Paul did not say "in these last days," as the writer of Hebrews did to refer to the whole church age (1:2). Paul used a different expression to convey the clear idea that the Holy Spirit is talking about the "later times" of the current church age. Therefore the Holy Spirit is giving a dual warning for the church in our day: first, "not to fall away from the faith," and second, don't pay "attention to deceitful spirits and doctrines of demons." We have already called attention to the problem of apostasy in the church today. The second warning is especially interesting in light of the fact that those within the church who depart from the faith are said to be especially open to demonic teachings.

We think it significant that both biblical terms for the demonic are used in this verse: "spirits" and "demons." A clear contrast is set up between what the Holy Spirit is explicitly saying as opposed to what "deceitful spirits" and "demons" are saying. The Holy Spirit's teaching that the "later times" will be characterized by apostasy in the church is strengthened by the addition of the term "explicitly," so that there is no mistaking what He is trying to say. However, many today in these "later times" who repeat this Spirit-inspired warning about the increase in apostasy are accused of being negative and divisive and of obstructing the work of the Holy Spirit. Yet at the same time these critics are teaching things which can be proved from the Bible to be error. This passage would lead us to believe that they are "paying attention to deceitful spirits and doctrines of demons." "Deceitful spirits" are the agents that Satan uses to generate these teachings, which are then said to be described as "doctrines of demons"—that is, doctrines that come from demons.

The Tragedy of Spiritism

This is illustrated in the life of King Saul in the Old Testament (1 Samuel 28). Early during his reign as king of Israel, Saul disobeyed God and strayed from the faith. God withdrew the ministry of the Holy Spirit, which gave guidance and direction to the king of Israel to know God's will in important matters of governing the nation. When Samuel died, Saul no longer had access to God's guidance for the nation. Toward the end of Saul's life he wanted to know whether he should engage in a battle with one of Israel's enemies, but God would not speak to him. In his distraught condition Saul turned from God and His clear warning in the law not to consult mediums (Deuteronomy 18:10-12), and he visited a medium in Endor so he could consult with Samuel. The next day God killed Saul and his sons in battle as a result of resorting to spiritism.

Too many people today are engaging in a form of "spiritual warfare" which involves carrying on conversations and discussions with demons. In fact, some are teaching as fact information which they have learned from demonic sources, whether explicitly from a demonic statement or implicitly from the way they operated. Some people are being told the names of demons, the hierarchical order of demons, and how many and which demons supposedly rule over certain territories.[7] Other examples of information learned from demons sometimes include what the demon is doing, why he is inhabiting a particular

7. Wagner and Pennoger, *Wrestling with Dark Angels*, pp. 76, 84-5.

person, his intents and purposes, and sometimes just general conversations. Since demons are liars and deceitful, how can anyone ever trust anything a demon would say? To engage in such practice is to come close to being involved in spiritism.

Walter Martin described spiritism as "the masquerade of demonic forces, who pretend to be departed spirits with the intent of deceiving through the power of Satan those foolish enough to believe the testimony of demons in preference to the authority of the Word of God Himself."[8] Since spiritism involves unauthorized communication with demons, this abomination is a very real possibility for those practicing the new spiritual warfare. This approach seems twice as risky in light of the many biblical warnings for believers to stay away from these kinds of things (Exodus 22:18; Leviticus 19:26,31; 20:6,27; Deuteronomy 18:9-12; Isaiah 8:19).

Demonic Dangers

Many of the current teachings on spiritual warfare promise great benefits to the church if followed. They promise a great hope in the area of evangelism: the greatest ingathering of souls in the history of the church. They also promise believers greater freedom and increased spiritual power. Unfortunately and tragically, when examined in the light of Scripture, this new spiritual warfare seems closer to fitting the description of the final apostasy during the end times of the church age. In addition, the new spiritual-warfare theology increasingly appears to fit the description of the false religious system headed by the false prophet in the coming tribulation period. It appears more than likely that Satan and his demons are giving many advocates of the new spiritual warfare the types of "power" experiences they are seeking in order to deceive them. Since these advocates tend to emphasize only the demonic realm (and that from a false perspective), they are open to Satan's attacks in the realm of the flesh and, especially because of lack of discernment, the influence of the world-system and its false teachings.

The apostasy of the last times during the church age leads up to and helps prepare the world for the coming false religion during the tribulation period. As we look at some of the passages describing characteristics of this final deception, it appears to us that many

8. Walter Martin, *The Kingdom of the Cults* (Minneapolis: Bethany Fellowship, 1965), pp. 199-200.

aspects of the new spiritual warfare are increasingly similar to the characteristics of this coming false religion. Notice that these characteristics which we are about to list could be called "occult sins." The false teachers are not noted for wanting to *take away* from the Word of God by denying God's Word, as evil as that error is, but for wanting to *add to* Scripture in the name of the Lord.

In Matthew 7:21-23 our Lord says, "Not everyone who says to Me, 'Lord, Lord,' will enter the kingdom of heaven" (verse 21a). This is followed by the response of the people excluded, who boasted of three activities which they thought should qualify them to go to heaven: "Did we not "prophesy in Your name, and in Your name cast out demons, and in Your name perform many miracles?" (verse 22). These are the very areas in which the new spiritual warfare claims achievements, and are major emphases in many of the teachings found within the new spiritual-warfare movement. However, our Lord's sobering reply was a command to depart from Him because "I never never knew you" (verse 23). According to Christ, true spirituality is evidenced not by power signs but by genuine Christian character (verse 20).

In 2 Corinthians 11:13-15 Paul warns believers that Satan and his demons are subtle and seductive in their dealings with Christians. Demons are able to disguise themselves as angels of light and servants of righteousness. Many people involved in the new spiritual-warfare movement give lip service to this notion, but seem open to information learned from any experience with the supernatural realm or any person who claims to speak in the name of the Lord no matter how much his teachings and lifestyle differ from those of the Bible.

The Final Apostasy

The apostasy of the last days is not a failure to believe in miracles. Instead, the apostasy will be characterized by an unbiblical emphasis on the miraculous and supernatural. A passage which describes this phenomenon is 2 Thessalonians 2:1-12. Paul states the future deception will include the following demonic activities: There will be a false spirit or message or letter (verse 2); there will be deception (verse 3,10); the deception will be persuasive because of the activity of Satan, which includes all power (miracles) and signs and false wonders (verse 9); God will send a deluding influence (verse 11).

Matthew 24:24 describes the tribulation period as a time to be on the lookout for "false Christs and false prophets" who "will arise and will show great signs and wonders, so as to mislead, if possible, even the elect." Notice that these *false* signs and wonders are called "great," which means that they are highly impressive displays. However, their purpose is to mislead, not to edify.

Revelation 13 includes a description of the religious false prophet who performs "great signs" (verse 13), which includes the ability to deceive "those who dwell on the earth because of the signs which it was given him to perform in the presence of the beast" (verse 14). This kind of occult power will be impressive to those who are not biblically discerning and who think that just because something is miraculous it must be of God.

The Book of Revelation describes the major reason for rejecting Christ during the coming tribulation as consisting primarily of occult sins. These include the worship of demons and idols as well as sorcery (9:20,21). In 16:14 we see "spirits of demons, performing signs, which go out to the kings of the whole world." Babylon the great is said to be "a dwelling place of demons and a prison of every unclean spirit" in 18:2. The world during the tribulation will be preoccupied with Satan and the demonic, but believers are supposed to be preoccupied with our Savior, the Lord Jesus Christ.

Victory with Christ

The Bible teaches that Christ Himself will gain the final victory over Satan at His second coming. Scripture also tells us that upon His return the saints will rule with Him in victory. This is made especially clear in the seven letters to the churches in Revelation chapters 2 and 3. These letters are written to church age believers and contain specific commendations which will be the basis for future rewards. Even here the Christian is seen as resisting the evil generated by Satan and the demonic by remaining true to the Lord in a defensive posture. Spirituality in the sight of God is measured by *holiness*, not power. The eternal rewards and positions of leadership are given on the basis of achieving true victory over the enemy by remaining faithful to the Lord's Word.

Revelation 2:25-27 is typical of what the Lord expects of His children. In Thyatira, believers are expected to "hold fast until I come" (verse 25). When Christ returns He will take believers to rule over the nations with Him (verse 26). This is something that is future, but future status is gained through present faithfulness to God and His Word. A similar promise is offered to Christians in Revelation 3:21.

The war will end with Christ Himself exercising victory over Satan and the demonic. What a glorious victory that will be! But we must not get trapped into thinking we can experience that victory in this age. In the current church age, the believer is called to evangelism and spiritual warfare on a threefold front: the world, the flesh, and the devil. We are not to *take dominion*, but to *stand firm*. We are not to *run the devil out of town*, but to *resist him*. As holy rebels we are called upon to resist the devil by focusing upon Christ until He returns from heaven and takes us home. This is the only way we can be truly effective as holy rebels.

— 12 —

Holy Rebels

Be strong in the Lord and in the strength of His might. Put on the full armor of God, that you may be able to stand firm against the schemes of the devil. For our struggle is not against flesh and blood, but against the rulers, against the powers, against the world forces of this darkness, against the spiritual forces of wickedness in the heavenly places.

—Ephesians 6:10-12

I (Thomas) recently heard a sermon by a nationally known televangelist. The sermon began with him looking into the camera and saying, "I rebuke you, Satan, and bind you by the blood!" I took out a piece of paper and divided it in half. Every time the televangelist made a reference to Satan and demons I noted it, and every time he talked about Christ I noted that too. It turned out that his sermon was not supposed to be about Satan but about the Christian life, yet this televangelist mentioned Satan and the demonic about twice as often as he did our Lord Jesus Christ! This kind of preoccupation with Satan is becoming all too common in Christian circles today.

We certainly believe that demonic activity is real and should be taken seriously, and in fact it is precisely because the Bible takes this subject seriously and gives specific instructions for dealing with the devil that we have written this book. Our goal is to help the church of Jesus Christ to look upon spiritual warfare from the perspective of God's infallible Word and not from the perspective of rationalism or experience.

The Bible views spiritual warfare as a conflict fought on three fronts: the world, the flesh, and the devil. Unfortunately, it is common today to major on Satan and demons while neglecting the other two fronts. We have seen that the enemy within, the flesh, is just as evil and is to be taken just as seriously as the worst demon from hell. Christians tend to be weakest in understanding how Satan influences them through his use of the world's thought system. It is in these areas of confrontation that holy rebels must be especially on their guard.

In the New Testament we are given a specific strategy for handling the attacks of the devil, whether by land (the flesh), sea (the demonic), or air (the world). This biblical framework is more than sufficient to equip us to resist Satan and to stand firm while enduring through prayer.

Now let's look at how to handle some of the situations noted in the opening chapter. You may want to read them again to refresh your memory about the details involved and the questions raised.

Answers to the Questions

In answer to the first question, pressures in life should be dealt with by realizing that holy rebels should act responsibly in every situation. If we give in to the pressures of the moment because of self-pity or other invalid reasons, we will never develop the type of resistance to the pull of the flesh and the voice of the world that we need in order to please the Lord. First Corinthians 10:13 assures us:

> No temptation has overtaken you but such as is common to man; and God is faithful, who will not allow you to be tempted beyond what you are able, but with the temptation will provide the way of escape also, that you may be able to endure it.

Sue was not looking to the Lord for deliverance from the situation. She had adopted the worldly thinking that she was entitled to certain pleasures even if this meant financial irresponsibility. All too many people have perpetuated ungodly habits by saying each time, "Just one more time."

In the second example, Jose and Maria are to be commended for wanting to see their friends and relatives come to faith in Christ. One can hardly pray too much, but it is possible to pray wrongly and for wrong things. God has made it clear in His Word that Satan and the demons will not be run out of town or from the earth until Christ and His angels accomplish this feat at the second coming. Jose and Maria should not be misled into thinking that we must sterilize an environment from the demonic before God can save people or bring revival.

Christ's strongest language during His earthly ministry was directed against "fine churchgoing people" who were just as blinded by Satan as demon-possessed people. Jesus told the religious leaders, "You are of your father the devil, and you want to do the desires of your father" (John 8:44). All unsaved people are in a sense equally blinded by Satan (Ephesians 2:2). God uses the same dynamics to save all people who are deeply into sin. There is no special gospel or unique approach for those who are demon-possessed.

Since Julia was a Christian she could not be demon-possessed. Satan and demons can influence a believer, but not against his will. Demons can tempt and exert influence, but each believer ultimately makes his or her own decision to sin or not to sin. Flip Wilson's famous statement "The devil made me do it" is biblically incorrect when applied to believers. The quick-fix solutions offered by deliverance teachings sound tempting, especially if we have struggled for a long time over a particular sin. However, this is not the biblical way. Usually a believer in this situation just needs to keep growing in his Christian life, since spiritual maturity equips a Christian to handle his problems in a godly way.

There is absolutely no indication from the Bible that a believer can be bound by occultic curses. Like Frank's friend, many people today are interpreting events in their life as the product of a curse. Yet if this were possible, the New Testament would have given us clear warnings and instructions on how to deal with such curses. (Interestingly, curses are common fears of those who traffic within the occult world.) The superstition that a Christian can be cursed and needs to have the curse discovered and broken before he can have spiritual victory is currently being taught in many Christian circles, but the Bible clearly teaches that we are in Christ and He protects us. Holy rebels should be concerned about the influence of the teachings and beliefs from the occult, but not about their spells. The same principle would apply to Fred and Linda's situation concerning the lady's worry about bringing a demon into the church.

In the fifth example, Carl should not participate in occult practices no matter how much they are said to be scientific or neutral, since they are based upon accepting false views of God, man, and change. In this area many Christians need to be warned: There are many motivational methods as well as psychological techniques which have their roots in the occult. These methods are often whitewashed by the use of neutral terminology, but this does not change their nature.

The only times the New Testament speaks about lust, murder, and anger, it is as a product of the flesh or sin nature. Bob and Bill would be wrong to interpret their problems as the product of evil spirits. We are clearly told in Scripture that "each one is tempted when he is carried away and enticed by his own lust" (James 1:14). Demons may be involved in the temptation process in the way an amplifier projects a voice, but the Bible teaches clearly that the flesh is our primary culprit.

Christ's payment for sin effectively deals with all sin in a person's life when he becomes a believer. To say that a person must go through a separate step of deliverance for occult sins, such as was told to Sandy, is not found in the Bible. Once again, superstition may suggest such a notion, but the Bible does not.

The Sure Word of God

We are calling on the body of Christ to reject the proliferating superstitions in Christendom. These beliefs are the products of human thoughts and experiences, but cannot be verified from the Bible. Possibly the fact that so many people have recently been converted out of the occult explains why spiritual warfare in many circles is increasingly resembling a "tit-for-tat" battle between two sorcerers. But the Bible says that our minds are to be renewed by *God's Word itself*, and not by the Word of God as interpreted from a non-Christian framework, especially a framework which has much in common with the occult.

As holy rebels we have been called to fight Satan and the demons through spiritual warfare, but our commissioning and orders come from Holy Scripture. The Holy Spirit, who wrote the Bible, does not say one thing in the written Word and then contradict Himself through a new teaching which is claimed to have come from the Holy Spirit. As Peter noted, "We have the prophetic word made more sure, to which you do well to pay attention..." (2 Peter 1:19). When there is a contradiction between human teachings and the Bible, we have no choice as holy rebels who have sworn allegiance to our Lord except to follow the sure Word of God. Won't you join us as we seek to faithfully serve our Lord and Savior, Jesus Christ, until He returns?

We've heard the call
of the Lord of Hosts:
Fight the good fight of faith—
Be strong in the Lord.
Gird your armor on
When your enemies assail,
For He is a strong deliverer
All power is given unto Him.
Go fight! Go fight!
Fight the good fight of faith.
—Author unknown

Questions or comments about the material in this book should be addressed to:

Biblical Awareness Ministries
P.O. Box 90014
Austin, Texas 78709

Biblical Awareness Ministries is jointly directed by Thomas Ice and Robert Dean, Jr. Six times a year they publish *Biblical Perspectives*. The cost of a yearly subscription is $10. A sample copy will be sent to all who enclose a self-addressed stamped, legal-size envelope.

Other Good Harvest House Reading

THE COURAGE OF A WOMAN
by *June Curtis*

We need strength to face personal tragedies, to guide rebellious children, to make business decisions with integrity, and to acknowledge personal failure. Often we need courage simply to wake up each morning to a complex and difficult world.

By drawing parallels between ourselves and people who faced similar difficulties in the Bible, June Curtis explores God's time-tested principles of courage and propels us toward a life of faith and hope.

CHRIST-ESTEEM
by *Don Matzat*

Going against the tide of psychology, Don Matzat says to forget self-esteem and instead learn to love, honor, and esteem Christ Jesus. If within yourself, you have discovered only emptiness, Matzat encourages you to discover a startling, yet solid, biblical truth: What you need is Christ-esteem, not self-esteem! When the search for personal identity hits a blind turn, Matzat points to the lasting identity that Christ offers.

THE MORAL CATASTROPHE
by *David Hocking*

With the deterioration of the traditional family, the rapid increase in drug, alcohol and sexual abuse, and the growing problems of the hungry and the homeless, Christians must start asking the questions that will result in answers. In this challenging look at the times we live in, author, Biola Hour teacher, and communicator David Hocking addresses the decline of morality in America and asks the hard questions that are required for our survival—from abortion, homosexuality, and pornography to the difficulties of the death penalty, Christian involvement in politics, and equal rights.

THE WAR WITHIN
by *Jay E. Adams*

Jay Adams, Christian counselor and bestselling author, describes the personal conflict with sin that rages within every true believer. Then with skill and understanding he exposes the enemy's principal tactics and spells out a clear biblical strategy for overcoming sin.

Dear Reader:

We would appreciate hearing from you regarding this Harvest House nonfiction book. It will enable us to continue to give you the best in Christian publishing.

1. What most influenced you to purchase *A Holy Rebellion*?
   - ☐ Author
   - ☐ Subject matter
   - ☐ Backcover copy
   - ☐ Recommendations
   - ☐ Cover/Title
   - ☐ ______________

2. Where did you purchase this book?
   - ☐ Christian bookstore
   - ☐ General bookstore
   - ☐ Department store
   - ☐ Grocery store
   - ☐ Other

3. Your overall rating of this book:
   ☐ Excellent ☐ Very good ☐ Good ☐ Fair ☐ Poor

4. How likely would you be to purchase other books by this author?
   - ☐ Very likely
   - ☐ Somewhat likely
   - ☐ Not very likely
   - ☐ Not at all

5. What types of books most interest you? (check all that apply)
   - ☐ Women's Books
   - ☐ Marriage Books
   - ☐ Current Issues
   - ☐ Self Help/Psychology
   - ☐ Bible Studies
   - ☐ Fiction
   - ☐ Biographies
   - ☐ Children's Books
   - ☐ Youth Books
   - ☐ Other ______________

6. Please check the box next to your age group.
   - ☐ Under 18
   - ☐ 18-24
   - ☐ 25-34
   - ☐ 35-44
   - ☐ 45-54
   - ☐ 55 and over

Mail to: Editorial Director
Harvest House Publishers
1075 Arrowsmith
Eugene, OR 97402

Name ______________________________________

Address ____________________________________

City ______________ State __________ Zip __________

Thank you for helping us to help you in future publications!